CONCORDE

CONCORDE

Günter Endres

MBI Publishing Company

First published in 2001 by MBI Publishing Company, Galtier PLaza, Suite 200, 380 Jackson Street, St. Paul, MN 55101-3885 USA

© Günter Endres, 2001

Previously published by Airlife Publishing Ltd, Shrewsbury England

MBI Publishing Company books are also available at discounts in bulk quantity for industrial or sales-promotional use. For details write to Special Sales Manager at Motorbooks International Wholesalers & Distributors, Galtier Plaza, Suite 200, 380 Jackson Street,
St. Paul, MN 55101-3885 USA.

Library of Congress Cataloging-in-Publication Data Available

ISBN 0-7603-1195-1

Printed in Singapore

PREVIOUS PAGE: 30th anniversary flight of Concorde from Filton on 9 April 1999.

BELOW: Head-on view of Concorde.

References

Costello, John and Hughes, Terry: *Concorde*; Angus & Robertson.

Gardner, Charles: *British Aircraft Corporation*; Book Club Associates.

Moon, Howard: *Soviet SST*; Orion Books.

Owen, Kenneth: *Concorde and the Americans*; Airlife.

Owen, Kenneth: *Concorde New Shape in the Sky*; Jane's.

Various Aérospatiale and British Aircraft Corporation (later British Aerospace) publications, *Russian Aviation, Air Enthusiast, Aviation Week & Space Technology, Flight International, Interavia*

Data tables

Accurate data for Concorde and other SSTs has been difficult to trace. Rather than inserting incorrect information in data tables, only data from reliable sources has been included.

CONTENTS

PREFACE

Numerous books have been written about Concorde, and only one I know of that covers the Tupolev Tu-144, the only two supersonic transports (SSTs) that made it into production and service. Volumes have been written about the political intrigues and dimensions in the race for a supersonic transport, and these are touched upon because they shaped the development of supersonics as much, if not more than the technological issues. But alongside the fascinating development of both these aircraft, there were many projects in Britain, France and the United States that never made it beyond the drawing board or the designers sketch pad. In this book I have, therefore, tried to pull together the different strands to provide an overview of the development of supersonic transport aircraft, and subsequent attempts, so far still-born, to produce a second-generation SST that draws on the considerable advances made in knowledge and technology.

Half way through my work, Concorde suffered its first accident while in service, necessitating unfortunate changes to the book to take account of this tragedy. I would like to take this opportunity to express my sorrow and condolences to the families and friends of the Air France flight and cabin crew, the 100 mostly German holidaymakers, and the four people on the ground, who all lost their lives. Because over the years Concorde has taken on iconic status, it was grounded and remains so at the time of writing this Foreword. One series of unforeseen events, which conspired to bring the aircraft down, does not make Concorde an unsafe aircraft, and I hope that by the time this book is published, this magnificent aircraft is back in the air where it belongs.

BELOW: Roll-out of British-assembled prototype 002 at Filton.

Acknowledgements

As author, only my name appears on the cover of the book, but with such a diverse subject, I had to draw on the expertise and goodwill of many companies and individuals. Of the two airlines operating Concorde, Air France was particularly helpful, both in London and Paris, and provided access to various heads of departments responsible for supersonic operations. I would particularly like to mention Anne Leroy-Sanguinetti, Pascal Moreuil, Edgard Chillaud, Hervé Page and Pasquale Monmarson-Fremont. British Airways assisted with photographs, as did Aérospatiale (now EADS Airbus). After much cajoling, BAE Systems also helped with photos. Colin Mitchell of Goodwood Travel filled in details of the many charter flights organised for Concorde. Boeing (and McDonnell Douglas before the take-over) provided excellent information on their most recent projects, while NASA Dryden Research Center filled in much detail on the experimental X-planes of the 1950s, as well as the more recent test flights with the Tu-144LL flying laboratory.

I would also particularly like to mention my long-standing friends Mike Stroud, for whom no request is too much trouble, and Dave Carter, who read and checked the technical content. Paul Eden, Gary Ransom, David Charlton, Adrian Meredith and Terry Shone were responsible for making available a large number of the photographs and illustrations. My heartfelt thanks goes to all of them.

Günter Endres
Lindfield, West Sussex
January 2001

1 THE SEARCH FOR SPEED

It was military expediency in World War II that initially created aircraft that could fly faster and higher than any before, and, more importantly, were designed to carry the new nuclear bombs, which raised the threat in both war and peacetime to a new level. The subsequent Cold War provided a clear opportunity and *raison d'être*, with Britain, the United States and the Soviet Union all entering the race to build the world's first supersonic bomber.

The quest for speed had been the central thread running through aircraft development ever since that famous day at Kitty Hawk, North Carolina, in December 1903, when Orville Wright made the first powered flight, more of a 12 second hop, in his Flyer biplane. Speed was soon appreciated in World War I, and later by the new commercial airlines, which began to shrink the world with aircraft gaining increasingly in speed and range. World War II, and the advent of the jet engine, pushed the frontiers still further and closer towards the magic, and as yet not fully understood, realm of the speed of sound.

War-time secrecy ensured that many early experiments received little or no attention until much later, when rocket- and jet-powered research aircraft had taken speed and altitude onto an entirely new level. Nevertheless, it is worth mentioning that in 1943, a Rolls-Royce Merlin 61-powered Spitfire PR Mk XI attained Mach 0.9 in a controlled dive from 40,000ft (12,192m), running the whole gamut of different aerodynamic responses as the aircraft entered and then pulled out of the transonic phase. Two years before, Britain's first jet, the Gloster E28/39 had made its first flight, and a Whittle engine, the Power Jets W2.700, was selected in 1943 as the power plant for the first supersonic project, the imaginative Miles M.52.

The M.52, a single-engined bullet-shaped aircraft with a jettisonable nose section and pressurised pilot compartment, resulted from the government-issued specification E24/43 for an experimental transonic aircraft intended to reach 1,000mph (1,610km/h, or about Mach 1.5). However, the aircraft was under-powered and no effective wing shape could be devised to operate efficiently in both the subsonic and supersonic regime. In February 1946, when the M.52 was nearly complete, the project was cancelled by the Ministry of Supply, ostensibly on the grounds that there was unacceptable risk to the pilot. The Ministry then shifted its emphasis to a transonic programme of air-launched models, and two years later, a scaled-down rocket-propelled unmanned version of the M.52 achieved Mach 1.4. Vickers also did much work with rocket-powered experimental pilotless transonic models.

By then, designers had begun to favour swept wings for supersonic flight over the conventional straight wings, having finally taken note of research published in Germany and the appearance late in the war of the swept-wing, rocket-propelled Messerschmitt Me-163 fighter, which could fly at Mach 0.8, if

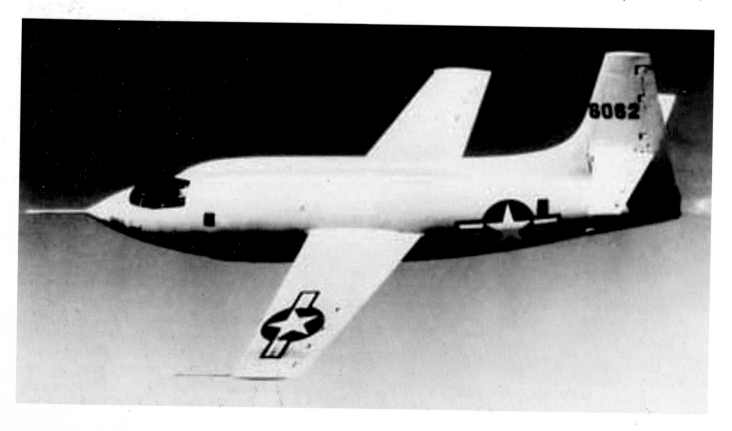

ABOVE: The Boulton Paul P.111 high-speed research aircraft on its first flight on 10 October 1950. The Nene-powered aircraft was capable of speeds of up to Mach 0.93 at 35,000ft (10,668m).

RIGHT: X-1-2 mounted under B-29 for launch. *NASA/Dryden Flight Research Center*

BELOW LEFT: Historic first recorded 'Mach Jump' by the X-1 on 14 October 1947. *USAF*

only for short periods. New research in Britain was begun with the de Havilland DH.108, a heavily modified Vampire fighter fitted with swept wings and a swept fin, but no horizontal tail surfaces. The first of three prototypes flew on 15 May 1948, and, after completing its trials to test the aerodynamic characteristics of the swept wing, was transferred to RAE Farnborough for other tests.

The second, much modified aircraft fitted with automatic slots, powered flying controls and increased sweep back of 45° was intended as a supersonic version to assess the high-speed characteristics of the wing. It quickly superseded the existing world speed record of 616mph (991km/h), but on 27 September 1946, the aircraft broke up due to the exceptionally heavy loads at a speed in the region of Mach 0.9, killing Geoffrey de Havilland Jr.

On 9 September 1948, de Havilland's chief test pilot John Derry became the first pilot in Britain to exceed Mach 1 during a test investigating transonic flight. In the 41-minute flight, Derry climbed to 40,000ft (12,192m) and achieved Mach 1.02 in a dive to 30,000ft (9,144m). By all accounts, he was lucky to survive.

THE MACH-BUSTERS

In the United States, the Research Airplane Program, a joint effort by the National Advisory Committee of Aeronautics (NACA), which later became the National Aeronautics and Space Administration (NASA) and the military services, was conceived near the end of World War II. Its purpose was to construct a series of special research aircraft to study the then unexplored transonic-low supersonic characteristics of full-scale aircraft in flight. The first of these, the radical bullet-shaped Bell X-1 with four-chambered Chemical Reaction Motors XLR-11 rocket engines, built for the United States Air Force (USAF) and NACA, was tasked to investigate the

LEFT: The X-planes: X-1A, D-558-1, XF-92A, X-5, D-558-II, X-4 and X-3. *NASA/Dryden Flight Research Center*

BELOW: Convair XF-92A in flight. *NASA/Dryden Flight Research Center*

BELOW RIGHT: North America A-5A Vigilante was a Mach 2 fighter. *NASA/Dryden Flight Research Center*

transonic speed range, and, if possible, break the sound barrier. This it managed to achieve on 14 October 1947, when USAF captain Charles 'Chuck' Yeager exceeded Mach 1, after being air-launched from under the bomb bay of a Boeing B-29 Super Fortress at 21,000ft (5,400m), and reached a speed of 700mph (1,126.5km/h) in level flight. Captain Yeager was also the pilot when the X-1 reached its maximum speed of 957mph (1,540km/h). Later growth versions of the X-1 included the X-1A, X-1B, X-1D and X-1E, which flew until 1958.

Next came the more conventional straight-winged Douglas D-558 I Skystreak, which was built for a joint US

Navy/NACA research programme, with a focus on stability, control and buffet investigations. Although the D-558 twice set world speed records, it went supersonic only once, achieving Mach 1.01 in a steep dive on 29 September 1948. This prompted the US Navy to claim it as the first supersonic flight, dismissing the air-launched X-1 as not qualifying as a real aircraft.

Douglas later built the swept-wing D-558 II Skyrocket, in which NACA pilot Scott Crossfield became the first man to fly faster than twice the speed of sound when he piloted the aircraft to a maximum speed of 1,291mph (2,077.6km/h) on 20 November 1953. The same aircraft also reached a record

altitude of 83,235ft (25,370m) on another flight. More X-planes followed, all exploring different parameters of flight. The Northrop X-4 had a low swept-wing and no horizontal tail surfaces, and was used to obtain data on the stability and control of semi-tailless aircraft at high subsonic speeds. It was also used to investigate stability problems at low speeds.

Bell's single jet-powered X-5 was the first swing-wing aircraft, capable of varying sweep angles from 20° to 60° at subsonic and transonic speeds. Results from these tests, which began on 20 June 1951 with the first flight, provided significant full-scale verification of wind-tunnel predictions for the reduced drag and improved performance resulting from the wing sweep as the aircraft approaches the speed of sound. Results also provided some input into the later design of the F-111 and the Navy's F-14 tactical aircraft.

The Convair XF-92A was the country's first delta-wing aircraft and had a speed of approximately Mach 1. Stability and control, pitch up and lift/drag measurements obtained from the XF-92A helped toward the technology that was used to develop such delta-wing aircraft as the F-102, F-106, B-58 and other high-performance machines. A slender fuselage and long tapered nose distinguished the Douglas X-3, which was also the first to investigate the design features necessary for sustained supersonic speeds. A secondary purpose was to test new materials such as titanium for aeronautical suitability.

The air-launched Bell rocket-powered, swept-wing X-2 marked a notable step up in capability — it was designed to fly three times faster than sound — but it proved a bridge too far. After one X-2 was destroyed in an explosion, the second aircraft went on to investigate aerodynamic heating and stability and control effectiveness at high speeds and altitudes. On 7 September 1956, Captain Ivan Kincheloe took the X-2 to an altitude of 126,200ft (38,466m). 20 days later, the X-2 programme ended when USAF Captain Milburn Apt piloted the aircraft to its highest speed of 2,094mph (3,370km/h) — over three times the speed of sound — before it went out of control and crashed killing its pilot.

Still greater speeds and altitudes were reached by the North American rocket-powered and missile-shaped X-15, which made a total of 199 flights, reaching flight maximums of 354,200ft (107,960m) in altitude, and a speed of 4,520mph (7,274km/h) or Mach 6.70. The X-15 flew for nearly ten years and made its last flight on 24 October 1968.

The last of the X-planes was the Rockwell XB-70, originally conceived as an advanced bomber for the USAF, but relegated to serve as a research aircraft. The world's largest experimental aircraft, powered by six General Electric YJ-93 turbojet engines, reached a speed of Mach 3.08 on 12 April 1966, and made its final flight on 4 February 1969. It was used to collect in-flight data for the design of future supersonic aircraft, both military and civil. It incorporated many of the features for sustained and efficient supersonic flight, including variable geometry intakes to control airflow to the engines, a thin swept delta wing (in the XB-70 the outer portion could be folded for greater directional stability), and a movable outer windshield for improved vision. The fuselage was constructed of rivetted titanium frames and skin, with most of the remaining structure built almost entirely of stainless steel.

FRENCH FLAIR

The French, later to join with Britain to build Concorde, also progressed through a series of supersonic research aircraft. It started with the Nord 1601, which first flew on 24 January 1950, and was built to investigate the stability of swept wings, the effect of sweep back on high-lift devices and other aerodynamic problems at high subsonic speed. Nord continued to build several more research aircraft, including the 1402 Gerfaut 1A, which was the first high-powered delta-wing aircraft to fly in France when it took to the air on 15 January 1954, and the 1500 Griffon, which followed on 20 September 1955.

The Gerfaut was capable of exceeding Mach 1 by the use of its 9,700lb (43.15kN) thrust SNECMA Atar 101G turbojets alone, without reheat or rocket assistance, but the Griffon employed a spectacular turbojet/ramjet propulsion unit to

ABOVE: The Avro 707 was a small delta-wing research monoplane powered by a single Rolls-Royce Derwent turbojet. In its 707A guise, it flew on 14 June 1951 and was used to explore high subsonic speeds. *Avro*

ABOVE RIGHT: One of several Myasishchev SST design proposals showing twin fins and large forward canards.

power it to Mach 1.85 (1,240mph/1,996km/h) in 1957. The turbojet was housed in a huge outer casing, which formed the ramjet used for high-speed flight, and was employed during low-speed flight and for starting the ramjet. However, while the aircraft was novel and successfully compiled test data on the airframe design for this turbojet/ramjet combination, ramjets proved relatively inefficient at the speeds reached and needed speeds of at least Mach 4 to come into their own. Interestingly, Concorde's first pilot, André Turcat, established an international speed record in the Griffon on 25 February 1959, and the following October reached Mach 2.19 (1,448mph/2,330 km/h), becoming the first European to fly above twice the speed of sound.

Meanwhile, Sud-Ouest (SNCASO) had built the straight-winged SO 9000 Trident, which first flew on 2 March 1953, and whose wing tip-mounted turbojets and a rocket buried in the fuselage propelled it to speeds of over 1,000mph (1,610 km/h) for the first time in January 1957. In 1956, the delta-winged Sud-Est (SNCASE) SE.212 Durandal reached Mach 1.5 on its first flight.

Dassault also contributed materially to supersonic knowledge with its Mirage Mach 2 high-altitude interceptor, and the earlier Mystère, which also later exceeded twice the speed of sound. Both entered into full-scale production. The swept-wing Mystère IVA first flew on 28 September 1952 with a 6,280lb (27.9kN) thrust Hispano-Suiza Tay turbojet, while the

succeeding Super-Mystère production version employed the higher-powered Atar 101G. The prototype, fitted with a Rolls-Royce Avon Ra.7, had exceeded Mach 1 on its fourth test flight on 3 March 1955. The delta-wing Mirage III, progenitor of many impressive developments, including trainers, long-range fighter bombers and reconnaissance versions, flew for the first time on 17 November 1956, also powered by the Atar 101G.

INTERCEPTORS TAKE OVER

All the time the data bank grew and the problems of supersonic flight were beginning to be better understood. The perceived threat from giant subsonic nuclear bombers under development in the Soviet Union in the early 1950s added yet another twist and gave rise to numerous designs for supersonic interceptors, with thoughts also turning to supersonic bombers. In Britain, Avro built the Model 707, a small delta-wing research aircraft, tasked to obtain data for its Vulcan high-altitude nuclear bomber. The Vulcan first flew on 30 August 1952, initially with four Rolls-Royce Avon Ra.3s, because the Bristol Siddeley

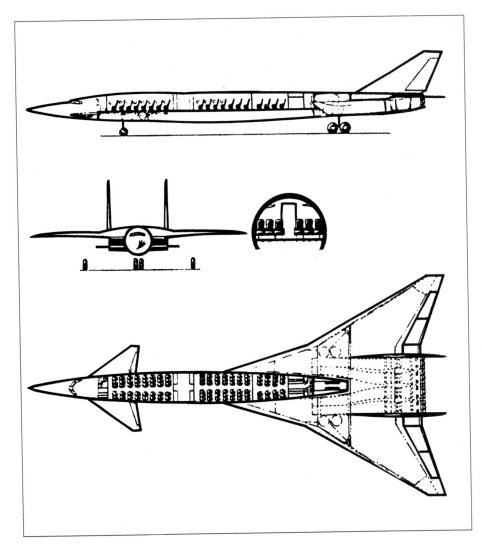

But Tupolev too was developing heavy bombers in parallel, having started work in 1952. Tupolev examined various wing shapes and the early sketch designs were built around these, in combination with new-generation turbojets then becoming available. Substantial progress was made, and on 30 July 1954, the Council of Ministers authorised Tupolev to develop and build a strategic supersonic bomber, as well as an unusual strike system, whereby a heavy bomber, designated Tu-108, was married to a smaller externally-mounted Tu-100 bomb-carrying aircraft. Under the '108' aircraft programme, large-scale research was undertaken into delta wing configuration, which later was put to good use in developing the first supersonic transport aircraft, the Tu-144.

In the UK Morien Morgan's Advanced Fighter Group had been set up in 1948, and two very different aircraft developed from that initiative. Both can be considered to have contributed greatly to the eventual development of a supersonic transport (SST). One of these was the Fairey Delta FD2, a tailless research aircraft with a delta wing, built to investigate the characteristics of flight and control at transonic and supersonic speeds. Two examples were built, powered by a Rolls-Royce Avon turbojet engine, the first of which made its maiden flight on 6 October 1954. On 10 March 1956, that same aircraft, flown by Peter Twiss, chief test pilot of Fairey Aviation, became the first to set a speed record above 1,000mph (1,609km/h), when a reheated Rolls-Royce Avon Ra.5 turbojet propelled the FD2 to the remarkable speed of Mach 1.7 1,132mph (1822km/h). This represented a considerable advance on the previous mark of 822mph (1,323km/h) set by a North American F-100 Super Sabre on 20 August 1955. The FD2 was later converted into the BAC 221 to carry on development flying for Concorde.

Olympus engine, for which it had been designed, was not ready. The second prototype, however, flew with 9,750lb (43.4kN) thrust Olympus 100 engines on 3 September 1953, and the Vulcan later played a major part in the development and testing of the Olympus engine for Concorde.

The first supersonic bomber was the Convair B-58 Hustler, first flown on 11 November 1956 and powered by four General Electric J79-GE-5B turbojets, which enabled it to reach speeds of up to Mach 2.1 (1,386mph/2,230km/h). On 26 May 1961, the Hustler set a world record of three hours 19 minutes and 58 seconds, flying from New York to the Paris air show at Le Bourget, covering the 3,628 miles (5,838km) distance at an average speed of 1,087mph (1,750km/h). Concorde later covered the same distance daily in around the same time, with 100 passengers aboard.

The Soviet bomber, which had instilled such fear into the Americans, was the four-engined Myasishchev Mi-4, first flown in late 1953. Built under instruction from Stalin, the Mi-4 was to have an intercontinental range to reach the United States, which in its Mi-4 Bison-B form eventually achieved that tremendous goal, but was by then already largely obsolete. Myasishchev followed up with another breathtaking aircraft, the supersonic M-50, said to have flown in late 1950s. Powered by four Koliesov turbojets, the Mi-50 underwent many changes, but is believed to have reached speeds of Mach 1.83.

The other aircraft was the English Electric P1A, one of three prototypes with swept wings and a tailplane, which exceeded the speed of sound on its first flight on 4 August 1954 and was later developed into the famous Lightning interceptor, which entered RAF service in December 1959. Much was learnt from the P1A flight tests about the variable exhaust nozzle on the Avon engine, a device necessary for an efficient reheat system. By then, supersonic interceptors proliferated, with several entering service in the United States, France and Great Britain, and bombers became less of a threat, because the development of missiles made them largely redundant. As a direct result, many research projects into bombers were abandoned. The exception was Britain's highly advanced supersonic tactical strike and reconnaissance bomber, the Mach 2.5 Olympus-powered TSR.2, which was started in 1959 and

ABOVE: Dassault Mystére IV.

LEFT: One of the two Fairey Delta 2 high-speed research aircraft (WG774) was converted into the BAC 221 with curved ogee wing for Concorde-related evaluation of high-speed handling characteristics.

made its first flight on 27 September 1964. Although brilliantly successful, it was killed off by the Labour Government on 6 April 1965. The same government had also tried the previous year to kill off the Anglo-French Concorde then under development, but luckily failed to do so.

SUSTAINED SUPERSONICS

Producing military aircraft, which were required merely to fly at supersonic speeds for short periods, was in comparative terms relatively simple. But building a civil airliner that could provide sustained supersonic flight for at least three hours at reasonable economics, made entirely separate demands on the airframe and engines.

So what is supersonic flight, and how does it differ from ordinary flight? Generally referred to as the Mach number (after Austrian physicist Ernst Mach), this is the ratio of the true airspeed to speed of sound in surrounding fluid, which varies with the square root of the air temperature. The speed of sound (Mach 1), therefore, decreases with increasing altitude through to the upper limit of the tropopause (around 36,089ft/11,000 m). Above that level, in the stratosphere where most aircraft fly, temperature and speed remain relatively constant. At sea level, under International Standard Atmosphere

(ISA) conditions, the speed of sound is approximately 760mph (1,225 km/h), while at 59,000ft (18,000m) it is some 100mph (160km/h) less. As the aircraft passes through the transonic phase, usually between Mach 0.8 and 1.2, there are marked changes in the airflow, which at around Mach 1.2 creates a cone-shaped shock wave, known as the Mach cone, as the air compresses. The resultant thunder-like sonic boom, or bang, heard on the ground is one of the seemingly intractable problems, which have so far prevented supersonic transports from flying across populated areas. For example, an aircraft flying supersonically at 50,000ft (15,240m) can produce a sonic boom 'carpet' about 50 miles (80km) wide, although it is most intense directly beneath the aircraft. The intensity of the sonic boom is influenced by weight, size and shape of aircraft, together with altitude, attitude, flight path and weather or atmospheric conditions. Ways of minimising the sonic boom to make it environmentally acceptable have yet to be devised, in spite of the intensive research undertaken to date and continuing.

In supersonic flight, the shock-wave pattern is accompanied by a sharp increase in aircraft drag, forcing designers to strike an acceptable balance (there is no perfect solution that provides efficiency at both flight regimes) between good control and handling characteristics at subsonic and transonic speeds, and the need for low drag in supersonic cruise. In Concorde, designers have achieved an effective compromise with lift/drag ratios of 7.7 in supersonic flight, and 12.8 in subsonic flight, giving only a marginally higher fuel consumption at subsonic speeds. Wind-tunnel research and flight testing have also established that the slender delta is the optimum shape for Mach 2 cruise. The pronounced sweepback keeps the wings within the nose shock-wave cone and the low aspect ratio minimises drag, while special cambers and tapers to the wing tips and leading edge improve low-speed controllability without detriment to the supersonic performance. The delta wing also boosts the formation of attached vortices in the airflow over the leading edges at low speeds and high levels of attack, providing increased lift in the landing phase and permitting the dispensation with high lift devices on the wing.

In addition to providing sufficient power for sustained supersonic flight of two hours or more, propulsive efficiency is also crucial to a successful supersonic design. The problems encountered in engine design for an SST stemmed from the fact that the airflow requirements of the engine vary considerably in the subsonic, transonic and supersonic phases of flight. The only answer is a variable geometry intake, which allows the air, at speeds at about Mach 1.3 and above, to be slowed down to subsonic speed and precisely meet the requirements of the engine. In Concorde, reheat has been employed to provide higher take-off thrust without a heavy weight penalty, and is also used during transonic acceleration, which, although using more fuel temporarily, cuts the overall fuel consumption by getting faster to supersonic speed at which consumption is at its lowest.

Another notable phenomenon of supersonic flight is that of kinetic heating, which has a major influence on the choice of materials for a supersonic aircraft. The boundary layer and the aircraft surface beneath are heated by skin friction, as it moves rapidly through the air, being roughly proportional to the square of the airspeed of Mach. The highest temperature occurs at the tip of the aircraft nose (about 127°C at Mach 2.2), but the temperature pattern varies across the surface, and is affected by speed and altitude. The stresses induced on the airframe due to the temperature difference between the skin and the air-conditioned interior of the aircraft have to be relieved and are a major aspect to be taken into account at the design stage. Concorde, for example, stretches by 6in (150mm) in flight. The choice of speed, therefore, governs which materials can be used for the structure. The temperature stresses generated at a speed of Mach 2.2 are about the limit for aluminium alloys generally used in subsonic aircraft construction. The use of titanium or similar high temperature resistant materials becomes necessary at speeds much in excess of Mach 2.2.

In sustained supersonic flight, aerodynamic, thermodynamic, atmospheric and structural factors interact in a complex pattern, not all elements of which were understood in the early days of supersonic research, nor have they yet been fully mastered. The designer was faced with a host of conflicting requirements, many of which were mutually incompatible and depended heavily on the choice of speed. Success was measured in devising a configuration that achieved an acceptable compromise between what was desired, and what was possible. Building a supersonic transport aircraft capable of carrying at least 100 passengers at twice the speed of sound, efficiently in all flight regimes, proved, therefore, a highly complex, but not insurmountable proposition.

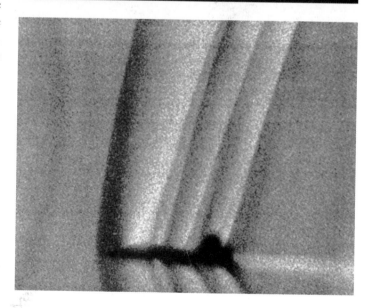

TOP AND CENTRE: The experience gained by Tupolev from the '108' research programme into delta-wing designs contributed greatly to the development of the Tu-144. Various wing shapes and engine configurations were examined, including these two six-turbojet designs from the 1954/55 period.

ABOVE: Schlieren photograph of a T-38 shock wave at Mach 1.1. *NASA/Dr Leonard Bernstein*

TOP RIGHT: The flight path to Concorde.

BELOW RIGHT: The Convair B-58 Hustler supersonic bomber flew from New York to Paris in a record time of just over three hours and 19 minutes, a time later achieved by Concorde in regular service between these two cities.

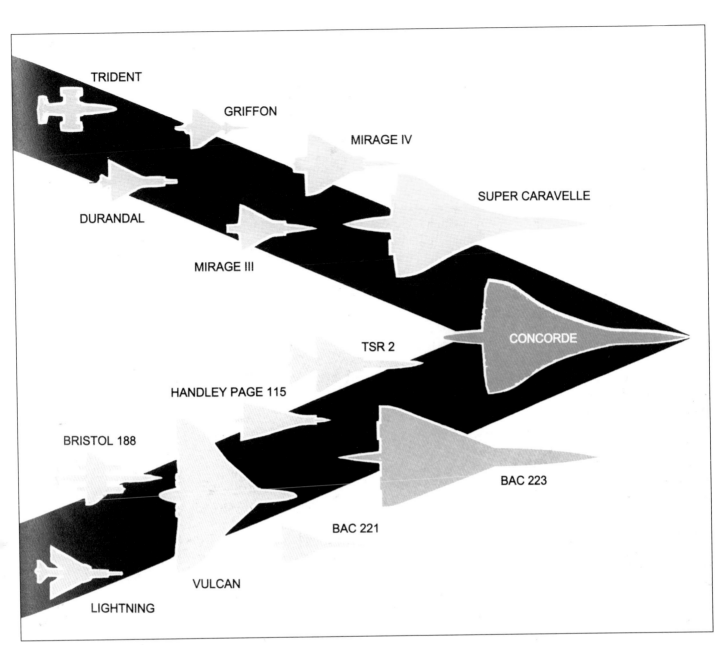

TRIDENT

GRIFFON

MIRAGE IV

SUPER CARAVELLE

DURANDAL

MIRAGE III

CONCORDE

TSR 2

HANDLEY PAGE 115

BRISTOL 188

BAC 223

BAC 221

VULCAN

LIGHTNING

2 EVOLUTION OF AN SST

Supersonic flight had opened up tremendous new possibilities, but the technology to produce a viable commercial supersonic transport (SST) with acceptable economics, still appeared out of reach. But technical answers were slowly evolving, both in Britain and France. A meeting at the Royal Aircraft Establishment (RAE) at Farnborough on 25 February 1954 under the chairmanship of the RAE's deputy director Morien Morgan attempted to bring some coherence to the divergent strands of supersonic thought. The conclusion was that a SST capable of flying 15 passengers from London to New York was indeed possible.

Farnborough's work on the straight-winged Avro 730 Mach 2 bomber (cancelled in 1956) served as the basis for commercial applications, with a transatlantic capability the first goal. However, by April 1955, designers concluded that new aerodynamic shapes, such as slender delta wings with controlled flow separation, needed to be explored and that an acceptable compromise between performance at supersonic and subsonic speeds had to be achieved. The latter premise gave rise to theoretical and wind tunnel tests of variable-geometry wings, although these were later discarded.

A formal research and design programme was agreed upon at a meeting in London on 1 October 1956, presided over by the then Ministry of Supply, and also including representatives of the aircraft industry, the two airline corporations BOAC and BEA, and the Ministry of Transport and Civil Aviation. The result was the establishment of a Supersonic Transport Aircraft Committee (STAC), chaired by Morien (later Sir Morien) Morgan, which was to base its work on the promising research undertaken at Farnborough. The aircraft industry was represented by seven airframe manufacturers (AV Roe, Armstrong Whitworth Aircraft, Bristol Aircraft, de Havilland Aircraft, Handley Page, Short Brothers and Vickers-Armstrong), and four engine companies (Armstrong Siddeley

Motors, Bristol Aero-Engines, de Havilland Engine Company and Rolls-Royce). Two further airframe manufacturers — English Electric and Fairey Aviation — joined the committee in November 1957. The two-year research programme produced 400 written papers and when the final report was submitted to the Ministry of Supply on 9 March 1959, the feasibility of the SST concept had been firmly established.

The STAC held its first meeting on 5 November 1956, when RAE scientists set up a preliminary research programme with the stated purpose 'to initiate and monitor a co-operative programme of aimed research designed to pave the way for a possible first generation of supersonic transport aircraft.' A technical subcommittee and seven specialist working groups were set up to implement the research programme. At that time, interest focused on two distinct types. One aircraft was to cover medium ranges, the other was to fly faster and further.

The outline requirement for the medium-range SST envisaged an aircraft capable of a cruising speed of Mach 1.2 and a range of 1,300 nautical miles (2,400km). The longer-range aircraft was targeted to fly 3,000nm (5,500km), sufficient to cross the Atlantic, at a cruising speed of Mach 1.8-2.0. Mach 2 was set as the upper limit, as conventional materials and structures could be used, while higher speeds would have required the development of new materials and construction techniques to permit operations at the higher temperatures.

BELOW: Evolution of the Bristol 198 from the modified M-wing design of 1957, to the final configuration featuring a low-mounted narrow delta and six engines. *Air Enthusiast*

TOP RIGHT: Large thin-wing Handley Page HP.109 configuration with eight engines.

BELOW RIGHT: One of the more interesting Bristol 198 proposals was this eight-engined high-mounted delta with a large gothic canard of October 1958. *Source: STAC Report*

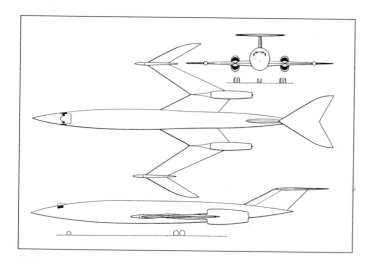

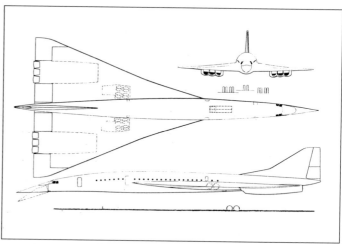

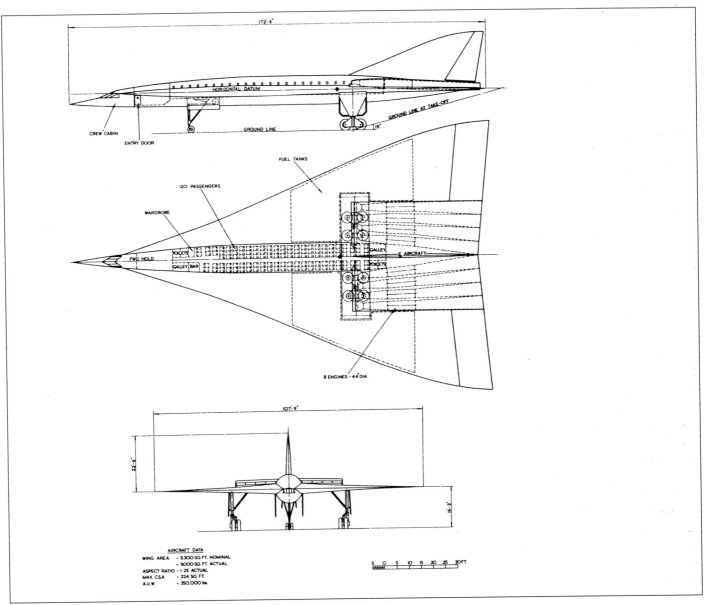

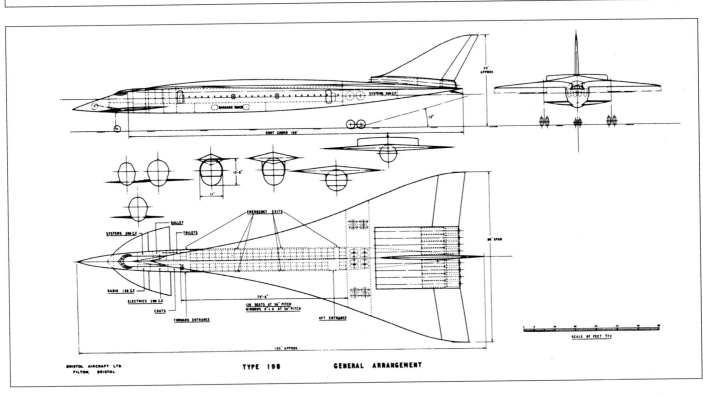

BRISTOL AIRCRAFT LTD.
FILTON, BRISTOL

TYPE 198

GENERAL ARRANGEMENT

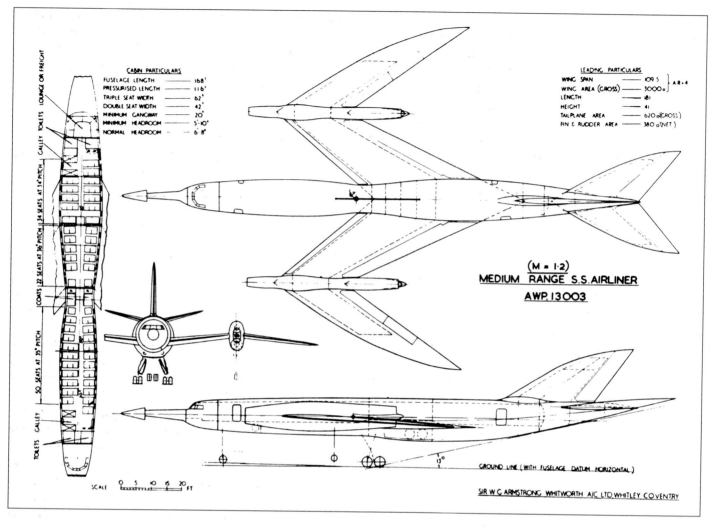

CABIN PARTICULARS

FUSELAGE LENGTH	168'
PRESSURISED LENGTH	116'
TRIPLE SEAT WIDTH	62'
DOUBLE SEAT WIDTH	42'
MINIMUM GANGWAY	20'
MINIMUM HEADROOM	5'·10'
NORMAL HEADROOM	6'·8'

LEADING PARTICULARS

WING SPAN	109·5
WING AREA (GROSS)	3000 □
LENGTH	181
HEIGHT	41
TAILPLANE AREA	620 □ (GROSS)
FIN & RUDDER AREA	380 □ (NET)

AR·4

(M = 1·2)
MEDIUM RANGE S.S. AIRLINER
AWP. 13003

GROUND LINE (WITH FUSELAGE DATUM HORIZONTAL)

SIR W G ARMSTRONG WHITWORTH A/C LTD. WHITLEY COVENTRY

SCALE 0 5 10 15 20 FT

Above: Medium-range M-shape Mach 1.2 proposal from Armstrong Whitworth attempting to reduce drag through 'area ruling', and deflect the supersonic shock wave away from the wings through the application of a special nose cone.
Source: STAC Report

Below: English Electric investigated a number of SST designs, including this P.30N model with an ogival wing and rear-mounted engines.

But major improvements were still required on the aero-dynamic front. Although using enhanced conventional shapes would have been technically feasible, it had been proved that the resulting aircraft would be highly inefficient. The most

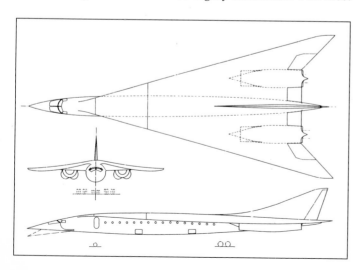

promise was shown by a slender delta wing, which offered the best solution at supersonic speeds, while the use of shock-free swept wings appeared best at subsonic speeds. For the slower aircraft, an M-shaped swept-back wing was considered, but when the medium-range aircraft was dropped, all effort was put into the slender delta design.

A variety of shapes were examined, including straight delta and gothic, the latter having a convex leading edge, but the ogee planform, which varies in curvature from concave to convex was later found to provide the best solution. But more detailed investigations discovered a problem of balance and stability, inherent in the slender delta wing, where the aerodynamic centre of lift moves aft as the speed increases and the aircraft has to be re-trimmed after take-off.

The difficulties of achieving stability by aerodynamic means led to early suggestions of transferring fuel between strategically located fuel tanks. Fully-integrated or all-wing designs, where the fuselage was wholly incorporated into a thick wing, also emerged and evoked strong differences of view for a time. In the end the disadvantages, primarily inefficient use of space, high friction drag and structural difficulties, were considered to outweigh the advantages and the idea was dropped.

The report of the STAC, formally presented to the Ministry of Supply on 9 March 1959, summarised the work that had been done, and illustrated three aircraft configurations selected from dozens of paper studies as the best candidates for further development. The committee strongly recommended that a long-range 150-seat SST should be built, with a stage length of 3,000nm (5,500km) for non-stop transatlantic operation. A cruising speed of Mach 1.8 (1,200mph/1,931km/h), which would enable a three hour journey time across the Atlantic, was suggested to avoid severe kinetic heating difficulties and permit the use of conventional aluminium alloys. Speeds in the region of Mach 2.6/3.0 were technically feasible, the committee added, but would imply 'major advances which would require considerable independent development, unless supported by work on an equivalent military project, and should be considered as the second generation of supersonic transports.' A smaller 100-passenger, Mach 1.2 aircraft with a full payload range of 1,300nm (2,400km), sufficient to cover a large part of Europe and domestic American routes, was also recommended.

'The two solutions on which most of our effort has been deployed,' the committee stated, 'form a basis for a sound engineering attack on the design of a supersonic transport aircraft.' It warned, however, that any delays in the development of an operational aircraft would seriously affect the aircraft's competitiveness. Based on a contract award by January 1960, it said, design studies could be completed by 1962, giving a target date for entry into airline service of 1971/72. The shorter-range version, the committee suggested, could be available two to three years earlier. Such optimism was backed up by two forecasts of the likely market for a supersonic transport around 1970. The Ministry of Transport and Civil Aviation estimated the demand at between 130 and 210 aircraft, while Vickers-Armstrong put the figure at between 300 and 500 aircraft. Both these predictions ultimately proved to have been widely off the mark.

Noting that development costs were 'difficult to estimate at this stage', the committee nevertheless indicated a highest cost of £95 million for the construction of six prototypes and the certification process. It also acknowledged that it would be 'difficult to bring the cost levels right down to those of modern long-range subsonic jets,' but believed that the economic gap 'will be progressively reduced in the next few years.'

DOWN TO THREE

The three aircraft configurations highlighted in the STAC report illustrated the wide envelope explored during the research programme, but represented only a fraction of configurations considered. Notable among these were the Avro 735, an eight-engined design developed from the Vulcan and proposed in November 1956, followed by the Avro 760 in November 1958. English Electric, which abstained from the early work of the STAC, also undertook various studies into SSTs between February 1959 and April 1960. Under the general designation of P.30, the company's projects covered speeds up to Mach 3, fixed and variable-geometry delta shapes, and four to six turbo-jet engines.

One such design was the P.30N, which proposed a unified wing/body arrangement with a high gothic delta wing. A design for the medium-range Mach 1.2 aircraft submitted by Armstrong Whitworth Aircraft (AWP.13003) showed a twin-engined design with an M-shaped gull wing attached on the centreline to a pinched fuselage, with the engines buried in the forward parts of the M. Handley Page's contribution to the STAC design studies included the Mach 1.8 long-range H.P.109, and the Mach 1.3 short-range H.P.110. The latter was proposed in both conventional and boundary suction variants, while one of the proposals under the H.P.109 designation was

BELOW: The most unusual (and impractical) proposal was the slewed wing concept from Handley Page.

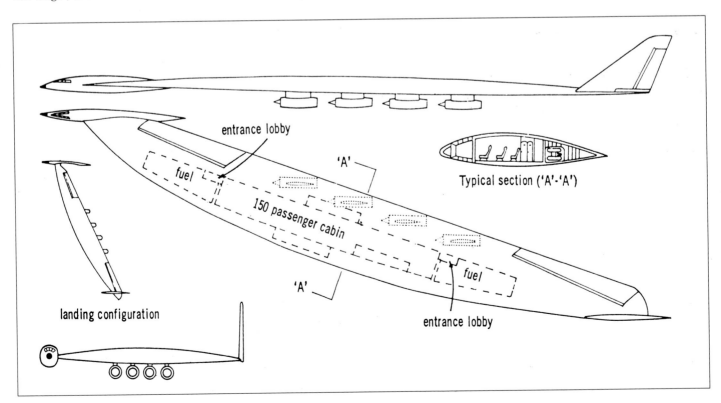

entrance lobby

fuel

'A'

150 passenger cabin

Typical section ('A'-'A')

'A'

fuel

landing configuration

entrance lobby

an all-wing aircraft with eight engines atop the wing, grouped towards the rear.

A brief study in 1961 examined the possibility of a large Mach 2.2 all-wing aircraft with the passengers accommodated within the wing, and four underslung podded turbojets in a novel rotating arrangement, which permitted the sweep angle to be varied. This 'slewed-wing' concept was quickly discarded, and Handley Page investigated only one more supersonic project, the H.P.128 short-range airliner, in early 1962. Designed to cruise at Mach 1.15 without causing a sonic bang at ground level, over stage lengths of 435 nautical miles, it was first proposed in a 90-seat layout, but later increased to 125 passengers. Studies continued until July 1964, but the company finally conceded that in spite of its speed advantage, such an aircraft would not be competitive with the larger subsonic types then coming into service. Sir Barnes Wallis, who could be relied upon to always apply original thinking to his designs, came up with the arrow-shaped Swallow, where the engines near the wing tips were hinged to effectively produce variable sweep, negating the use of aerodynamic control surfaces. A retractable cockpit was proposed to keep drag down in flight. It is difficult to see, however, how this novel arrangement could have been made to work.

The general arrangement that attracted most attention was the Bristol Type 198, dating from October 1958 and aimed at the North Atlantic market, which projected an eight-engined slender delta with a high-mounted ogee wing and a large canard foreplane. Earlier designs under the same designation had included a medium-range SST with a modified M-wing layout, with vertical pairs of wing-mounted engines and a slender waisted fuselage, but subsequent investigations concentrated almost entirely on long-range designs.

As illustrated in the STAC report, the Type 198 was 314,000lb (142,430kg) aircraft with eight 15,400lb (66.75kN) thrust engines sitting atop the wing, four on each side of the tailfin. It could carry 120 passengers for the required distance of 3,000nm (5,550km). Use of a blown flap on the canard was required to provide a nose-up moment when the trailing edge 'flaperons' were selected down for landing. The canard flap was also used for pitch control during cruise. A later configuration used a gothic wing without canards, and six turbojet engines in a similar location.

BELOW: The Bristol 221, a converted Fairey Delta 2 with slender ogee wing, to gain experience of high-speed handling.

While the STAC report was being considered, the Ministry of Supply placed a contract with Bristol Aircraft to prepare a comparative structural design study for a Mach 1.8 light alloy aircraft, against a Mach 3 steel and titanium version given the type designation 213. High costs and the lengthy development period needed later ruled out the faster aircraft. In September 1959, Bristol and Avro were asked to undertake a joint feasibility study into the most suitable design for a long-range SST, using both the Type 198 and the very different Avro 735 as starting points. What emerged from these studies in January 1960 was a considerably changed Bristol 198, now with a low wing, narrow delta configuration without canards, and six Olympus 591 turbojets grouped three-a-side in nacelles under the wing.

It was felt that this new design came closest to a perceived optimum solution, and a follow-on contract for continued studies was received in October 1960. By then, the consolidation of the British aircraft industry had been initiated with the formation of the British Aircraft Corporation (BAC) through the merger of Bristol, English Electric and Vickers. When BAC submitted its new proposal under the latest contract in August 1961, few changes had been made from the January 1960 design. In its final configuration, the Type 198 was to be powered by six 26,700lb (119kN) thrust Bristol Siddeley Olympus 593/3 engines. The gross weight was 385,000lb (174,600kg), and range with a maximum payload of 33,000lb (14,970kg) was a slightly longer 3,260nm (6,000km). It was sized to carry 136 passengers at a seat pitch of 33in (84cm).

In the endeavour to find aerodynamic solutions to supersonic flight, the matter of the sonic boom had not received the highest priority. In its report, the STAC concluded that 'the intensities of sonic bangs that the public will tolerate will have to be found by experience, but there is a good chance that the restriction of supersonic flight to altitudes above 35,000ft should be acceptable.' It did concede, however, somewhat prophetically as it turned out, that if not acceptable, acceleration to supersonic speed 'must be delayed a short time until the aircraft is over the sea.' As the Type 198 evolved into a large and heavy transport, doubts about the acceptability of the sonic boom began to grow.

There were also concerns about the economics of a six-engine installation, and the intake design still caused problems. In response, BAC produced an alternative scaled-down design with only four Olympus 592/3 engines, a gross weight of 260,000lb (117,935kg), and seating for a maximum 110 passengers on the London–New York route. By the end of 1961, the Type 198 had been abandoned in favour of the smaller Type 223.

On the other side of the Channel, French design activity for a supersonic transport cranked into gear at the beginning of 1957, when the government issued an outline requirement to industry based on an Air France specification for a medium-range SST carrying 60-70 passengers over a distance of 1,900 nm (3,500km). The French national airline wanted to maintain the momentum of the success achieved with the subsonic Caravelle twin-jet but, unrealistically, expected the same operating costs for the supersonic development. The three main manufacturers — Nord-Aviation, Sud-Aviation, which had been formed that year through the merger of Sud-Est and Sud-Ouest, and Marcel Dassault — immediately began independent design studies for an SST. Sud-Aviation and Dassault appeared to be taking a similar approach, and in early 1960, the two manufacturers combined resources to make a joint submission. Nord Aviation dropped out of the competition.

By mid-1961, the Bristol studies and those carried out in France by Sud-Aviation, had reached almost identical conclusions as to size, configuration and performance parameters for a possible supersonic transport. The next logical step, therefore, was to merge the two programmes into a single project, a process that appeared relatively simple and had the backing of politicians on both sides of the Channel. In fact, in the design contract awarded to Bristol Aircraft and Avro in September 1959, the Ministry of Supply had already suggested that possible collaboration with manufacturers in France, Germany and the United States should be explored.

US FALLS AT FIRST HURDLE

Only France took up the offer of a risk- and cost-sharing partnership. Germany's industry was not then ready for such a major venture, and the US spurned the British approach for a joint development in order to go one bigger and faster. But in spite of the support of successive presidents, the US project was soon floundering in the quagmire of Congressional machinations and growing environmental opposition. This was compounded in March 1971, when Congress finally killed off the programme by refusing to sanction any more public funds.

But the long road leading up to this final death knell started with a specification that was far too ambitious. By setting a target of Mach 3, the designers were faced with a journey which would take them largely into the unknown, both from an aerodynamic and structural standpoint. These challenges would, of course, have been overcome, but not in the timeframe set, a fact that had been acknowledged very early on by both the British and French designers.

The US had begun looking into the possibilities of producing a SST on the back of military bomber developments since the late 1950s. Convair came up with a far-fetched proposal to convert the B-58 Hustler into an airliner carrying 40 passengers in a detachable pod, and also offered a modified version as a supersonic presidential transport. In June 1959, Lockheed presented a design for a Mach 3 SST to the Institute of Aeronautical Sciences in Los Angeles, which became much talked about. But it was the presidency of John F Kennedy that moved the plans forward. In July 1961, a steering committee was formed with members from the Federal Aviation Agency (FAA), the National Aeronautics and Space Administration (NASA) and the Defense Department, and the following month, Congress approved US$11 million for preliminary research. A subsequent study commissioned by the president from the FAA called for the 'earliest production' of a Mach 3 SST, and proposals went out to industry to come up with appropriate designs within two years. The programme was being overseen by the Supersonic Transport Advisory Group (STAG), which, in December 1962, alarmed at the progress being made in Europe, recommended that a US SST must be built if Europe was not to achieve an unassailable lead. News filtering through from Moscow that the Soviet Union had also entered the race (see Chapter 6) added to the concern, and this was increased still further with the announcement on 4 June 1963 that Pan American World Airways had placed options on six Concordes.

The timing of the Pan Am announcement was deliberate and had the desired effect. The next day, President Kennedy committed the US Government to the construction of a bigger and better SST. He sent a clear message that he expected Congress to back him saying that it 'should be prepared to invest the funds and the effort necessary to maintain the national lead in long-range aircraft.' As in the USSR, prestige and national pride had overruled commercial considerations.

On 15 August 1963, the Federal Aviation Administration (FAA) invited bids from the American industry to begin SST work in earnest, as Kennedy wanted to have an American supersonic transport flying across the Atlantic by the time he planned to have a man on the moon. The initial, highly unrealistic timescale, therefore, envisaged having a prototype in the air by late 1967, but the schedule continued to slip. The assassination of Kennedy in November 1963 cast a shadow over the programme, but by then, the juggernaut had gained momentum and it was too late to call a halt. As yet, nothing concrete had emerged from the design teams, but US airlines

rushed to put down deposits, headed by TWA and followed immediately by Pan American and others. By the beginning of 1964, the US SST had attracted options for 63 aircraft, compared to 37 for Concorde. The decision by BOAC to add six US SSTs to its Concorde options did not go down well in Britain.

Sketchy design proposals, based on carrying 160 passengers at a minimum speed of Mach 2.2 a distance of 4,000 nautical miles, were submitted by industry in January 1964, but proved disappointing. These included the Boeing swing-wing Model 733, the North American NAC-60 with a conical-camber modified-delta wing and fixed forward canards derived from the triple supersonic B-70 Valkyrie strategic bomber, and the double-delta Lockheed CL-823. Further design and research work was then authorised by President Lyndon B Johnson, an ardent SST supporter since his days as vice-president under Kennedy, with design contracts awarded in June. In July 1965 an 18-month design competition was ordered, and Boeing and Lockheed submitted their proposals in September 1966. Problems with the B-70 prompted North American to pull out.

Boeing used a full-size mock-up of its Model 2707-100 (a much modified 733) in a glitzy Hollywood-style presentation to impress the judges assembled on 23 September. The Model 2707-100 was a variable-geometry aircraft, designed to provide efficient operation at both subsonic and supersonic speeds, carrying up to 350 passengers over intercontinental distances at a cruising speed of Mach 2.7 (1,800mph/2,900km/h).

COMPARISON OF US SST SPECIFICATIONS

	BOEING 733	B2707-300	LOCKHEED 2000-7	NAC 60
Wingspan max	98ft 5in (30m)*	142ft (43.27m)	116ft (35.36m)	121ft 4in (36.98m)
Length overall	271ft (82.60m)	287ft (87.47m)	260ft (79.25m)	195ft 5in (59.56m)
Height overall	45ft 3in (13.79m)	50ft (15.24m)	47ft 11in (14.60m)	48ft 3in (14.70m)
Wing area, gross	5,019ft² (466.3m²)	8,497ft² (789m²)	9,026ft² (838.5m²)	6,417sq.ft (596.1m²)
Power plant	4 x GE4/J	4 x GE4/J	4 x GE4/F or P&W JT11	
Typical accommodation	250 passengers	250 passengers	250 passengers	170 passengers
Max T-O weight	500,000lb (226,800kg)	635,000lb (288,030kg)	480,000lb (217,720kg)	
Normal cruise	Mach 2.7	Mach 2.7	Mach 3.0	Mach 2.65
Max cruising height	65,000ft (19,800m)	70,000ft (21,335m)	80,000ft (24,400m)	
Typical range	3,480nm (4,000 miles/ 6,440km)	3,480nm (4,000 miles/ 6,440km)	3,480nm (4,000 miles/ 6,440km)	3,480nm (4,000 miles/ 6,440km)

* 72° sweep, wingspan with 20° sweep is 169ft 3in (51.59m)

BOEING SST DESIGN SPECIFICATIONS

	MODEL 2707-100 (9/1966)	2707-200	2707-300 (11/1968)	2707-300 (PROTOTYPE)
Wingspan	53.10m (174ft 3in)	177ft 5in (54.07m)	141ft 8in (43.18m)	142ft (43.27m)
Sweep	20° – 72°	20° – 72°	50° 30'	50.5°
Wing area	9,000sq,ft (836.1m²)	7,700sq.ft (715.3m²)		
Length	306ft (93.27m)	298ft (90.83m)	280ft (85.34m)	287ft (87.47m)
Height	46ft 3in (14.10m)	53ft (16.15m)	50ft 1in (15.26m)	50ft (15.24m)
Power Plant	all 4 x 267kN (60,000lb) GE4/J			
Accommodation	277	292	234	250
Gross weight	675,000lb (306,175kg)	680,000lb (308,440kg)	710,000lb (322,050kg)	750,000lb (340,200kg)
Cruise speed	Mach 3.0	Mach 3.0	Mach 2.7	Mach 2.7
Cruising altitude	64,000ft (19,500m)	64,000ft (19,500m)	64,000ft (19,500m)	60-70,000ft (18,290-21,335m)
Range	4,000 miles (6,440km)	4,000 miles (6,440km)	4,000 miles (6,440km)	4,000 miles (6,440km)

Maximum take-off weight was set at 675,000lb (306,175kg). The outboard section of each wing was designed to swing about a single pivot to provide a 20° leading-edge sweep for landing, a 30° sweep for take-off, and a 72° sweep for supersonic cruise, with an intermediate angle for subsonic cruise. In the supersonic configuration, the wing integrated with the large tailplane to provide a single lifting surface. The variable-geometry wing was designed with extensive high-lift devices, including slotted Fowler trailing-edge flaps and leading-edge slats along 85 percent of the span. Lateral control at low speeds was to be provided by conventional ailerons, with pitch control via inset elevators and pivoted tailplane tips. The latter were to provide sole lateral control when the wings were fully swept.

The tailplane supported four General Electric GE4 turbojet engines, each rated at 60,000lb (267kN) static thrust with afterburners and suspended in individual pods. All were provided with variable inlets and exhausts. 'Soft' touchdown characteristics were to be achieved with two staggered pair of four-wheel main bogies, plus a twin-wheel nose unit. Most of the structure was comprised of an alloy of 90 percent titanium, 6 percent aluminium and 4 percent vanadium. The 2707-100 was overweight from the start, and the problem was only partially alleviated in the -200 model, which also had a canard added to improve low speed handling.

In sharp contrast, Lockheed, partnered by Pratt & Whitney, had taken heed of the European approach and presented a much simpler and more economic design, now known as the L-2000-7, also in a full-size mock-up form. Powered by the JTF17A-20L turbofan (the GE4/J5K with reheat was an alternative), the L-2000-7 design had a thin double-delta wing with twist and camber. The only movable surfaces were elevons for pitch and roll control on the trailing edge, with simple hinged leading-edge flaps.

The outline specification provided for a cruise at Mach 2.7, a typical passenger load of 255, and a range of 4,000 statute miles (6,437km). Maximum projected take-off weight was 500,000lb (226,800kg). All but a small proportion of the structure was to be of titanium alloys, with the remainder of stainless steel. This configuration was believed to have given the company the edge over its great rival in Seattle, even though the Boeing design was considered more advanced. Final evaluation of the

BELOW: Tests in the hydrodynamic tunnel show the intricate patterns of airflow over the slender delta wing.

ANATOMY OF THE BOEING SST

1. Movable forebody hinges downward to give pilots added visibility at subsonic speeds.
2. Flight deck.
3. Entry door.
4. First-class passenger seats, four-abreast.
5. Nose gear.
6. Stowage console.
7. Galley units.
8. Six-abreast tourist class passenger seats (extend aft to cargo retaining bulkhead.)
9. Lower-deck cargo compartment.
10. Body frames.
11. Leading-edge slats.
12. Ribs.
13. Floor beams.
14. Pressure web structure.
15. Fuel tank.
16. Main landing gear well.
17. Wing pivot.

18. Outboard wing section pivoted forward to 30° sweep.
19. Flaps.
20. Spoilers.
21. Aileron.
22. Wing sweep actuator.
23. Main landing gear well.
24. Engine.
25. Cargo retaining bulkhead.
26. Cargo door.

27. Main deck cargo compartment.
28. Elevon.
29. Elevator.
30. Pressure bulkhead.
31. Ventral fin.
32. Fin.
33. Tail cone.
34. Emergency exit.

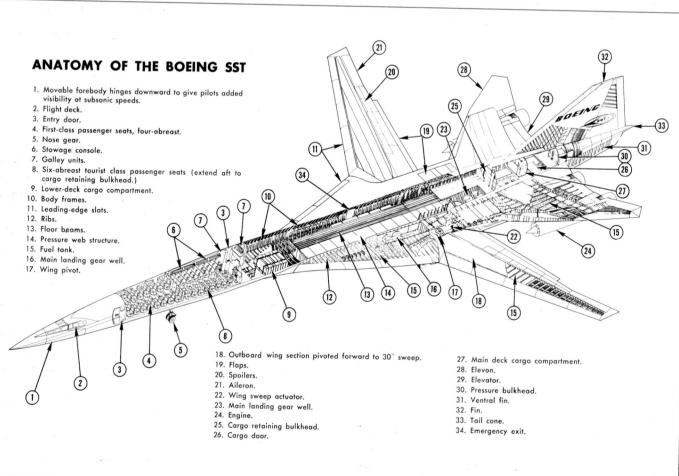

two designs was begun in September, but, to the surprise of many observers, on 31 December 1966 Boeing was announced as the winner of the competition for the design and development of America's first supersonic transport aircraft. However, President Johnson did not give the go-ahead until 29 April 1967, after receiving prior assurance sought from the US airlines holding delivery positions to contribute US$1 million each in risk capital. The total cost of the development was then put at US$1,444 million.

A contract for two prototypes was signed on 1 May 1967, retroactive to 1 January. But Boeing soon found the technical problems mounting and in February 1968 requested more time to begin a comprehensive re-evaluation of the variable-sweep design. By July, it had whittled down 16 contending designs to just three, the variable-sweep Model 969-404, the 969-321 with a highly-swept, cambered and twisted arrow wing planform with foldout canards for take-off, and the conventional delta 969-302. The variable sweep concept was still the focus, but it was not long before Boeing finally admitted defeat, announcing a new design, the Model 2707-300, on 8 December. This discarded the swing-wing concept and opted for a simpler fixed-delta design (based on the 969-302), which, in general outline was not dissimilar to Concorde. It came also close to the original but losing Lockheed design, a fact that did not go down well with the people at Burbank.

The Model 2707-300 was proposed to the FAA in January 1969 and the new President Richard Nixon, in spite of receiving negative feedback from a committee he set up on 29 January to investigate the programme, gave the go-ahead on 23 September. By that time, flight testing of both Concorde and the Tu-144 were already underway, and with Concorde then planned to go into airline service in 1972, its lead over the US SST had stretched to over five years, leading to a re-assessment of the potential market.

But delays and market considerations aside, the programme was already in deep trouble. Costs were escalating to such an extent that opposition grew in Congress, led by Wisconsin Senator William Proxmire. The environmental lobby, focused on the Citizens' League Against the Sonic Boom, also grew stronger by the day. In April 1970, the SST programme was transferred from the FAA to the Department of Transportation and put in the hands of William Magruder, who, over the following months, made desperate efforts to present a strong case for the SST, which by then had received 122 commitments from 26 of the world's leading airlines. But, although Congress had voted to continue funding in May, the US Senate in a crucial vote on 3 December 1970 rejected further expenditure on the project. After much congressional manoeuvring a compromise was reached under which SST funding was extended to 31 March 1971.

Boeing also issued various press releases extolling the virtues and necessity to proceed with its SST. The US SST can capture about $20 billion of the estimated world market of $25 billion up to 1990 it argued, adding that even if it is behind now, 'we will be competitive because the US SST will carry more than twice as many persons 400 miles an hour faster.' It

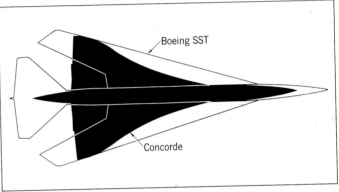

TOP: One of the early Boeing designs under the general 733 designation.

ABOVE: Size comparison between Concorde and the proposed Boeing SST.

TOP LEFT: North America examined a number of designs, including this variant with twin tails and large forward canards.

BELOW LEFT: Anatomy of the Boeing 2707 swing-wing design, before the company changed to a fixed delta.

referred to the lead the Comet had over the 707 in the 1950s, yet, it said, within two or three years the 707 and DC-8 had taken the major share of the market, because 'the US builds a better, more efficient airplane.' That arrogance was quite staggering, but turned out to be mere bravado, when in the same breath it warned of the possibility of a second-generation Concorde. This, Boeing contended, could offer comparable performance and threaten the potential market unless the US keeps with the schedule, which would provide commercial service in 1978. But it was all in vain.

On 18 March 1971, the House of Representatives voted to delete all SST funds, confirmed six days later when the US Senate defeated an amendment to restore the funds. The 'paper' American SST, on which more than $1 billion and 8.5 million man-hours had been expended, was dead. But the social cost was even more horrendous. 7,000 Boeing workers were laid off immediately, with another 6,000 at engine maker General Electric, but the repercussions were felt right across America. It proved an expensive burial.

3 DESIGN AND CONSTRUCTION

With Germany disinterested and the US determined to go it alone, only France looked a realistic prospect for a partnership. Given the SST work carried out in France and the obvious convergence of the designs, it was also the most logical solution. A visit by the British Minister of Aviation, Duncan Sandys, to France paved the way for tentative exploratory discussions in April 1960 between Bristol Aircraft and Sud-Aviation, led by technical director Pierre Satre. The Bristol Aircraft team was headed by technical director Dr (later Sir) Archibald Russell and chief designer Dr William Strang. The meeting laid the groundwork for a possible collaboration, but both companies continued independently on their respective designs.

The unexpected display at the Paris Air Show in May 1961 of a model of the Super Caravelle SST, which exhibited remarkable similarities with the Bristol 223, galvanised the two companies into action. The first official meetings between Bristol (now part of the British Aircraft Corporation) and Sud-Aviation were held in Paris on 8 June and at Weybridge on 10 July, and for the first time, the adoption of a single design and a pooling of resources were discussed seriously. Progress was also being made on the likely engine for the SST, with Bristol

Siddeley and Société Nationale d'Etudes et de Construction de Moteurs d'Aviation (SNECMA) signing a formal agreement for co-operation on 28 November 1961.

The impetus created by the industry was taken up at government level and taken one step further in a meeting between Peter Thorneycroft, British Minister of Aviation, and Robert Buron, the French Minister of Public Works and Transport, in Paris. The outcome was a formal request to both BAC and Sud-Aviation to come up with a joint project.

That was easier said then done, with BAC insisting that only a transatlantic-capable aircraft was viable, and Sud-Aviation equally determined to persist with a medium-range design, often leading to heated discussions. Nevertheless, in a review meeting at Suresnes, Paris, on 17 January 1962, attended by Dr Russell and Dr Strang of BAC and Pierre Satre and Lucien Servanty of Sud-Aviation, the two companies agreed to jointly proceed with both versions. The drawings submitted at that meeting showed identically sized aircraft, both with four Bristol-Siddeley Olympus 593 turbojets, the only major difference being additional fuel tanks for the long-range variant. At a further meeting between Thorneycroft and Buron on 26

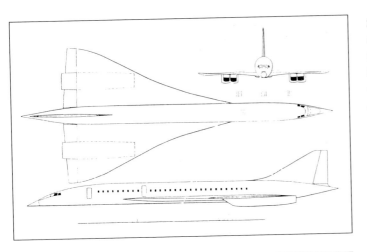

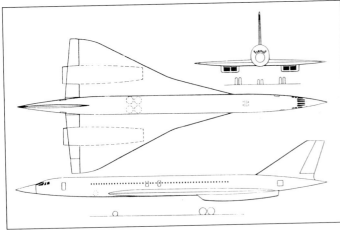

ABOVE: The similarities of the Bristol 223 and the Sud-Aviation Super Caravelle led to the merging of the two projects into Concorde. *Air Enthusiast*

LEFT: The model of the Sud-Aviation Super Caravelle at the Paris Air Show in 1961. *Air Enthusiast*

March, the Ministers decreed that these preliminary designs would serve as the basis for an Anglo-French supersonic airliner. While the governments hammered out the political and commercial details for a 50/50 programme split, the two companies were told to refine their designs and undertake other preparatory work 'to enable the governments to reach a decision.'

A more detailed specification for the as yet unnamed aircraft was completed and incorporated in an agreement exchanged by BAC and Sud-Aviation on 25 October. The historic Anglo-French Supersonic Aircraft Agreement 'to develop and produce jointly a civil supersonic transport aircraft' was then signed in London on 29 November 1962 by Britain's Minister of Aviation, Julian Amery, and the French ambassador, Geoffroy de Courcel. The seven articles in this momentous agreement laid down the principles of the collaboration between the two countries. These provided for the equal sharing, on the basis of equal responsibility, of the expenditure incurred by the two governments for development and production of the whole project (including airframe, engine, systems and equipment), as well as the proceeds of sales. The agreement also confirmed that both medium- and long-range versions were to be developed, making the point that equal attention was to be paid to the two types. At the same time, approval was

given for the agreements reached between BAC and Aérospatiale, and between Rolls-Royce and SNECMA, and the setting up of integrated organisation of the airframe and engine firms. A Standing Committee of officials from the two countries was to supervise the work and ensure that the programme was carried out in accordance with the provisions of the agreement.

FRENCH 'NON'

Britain had hoped that this historic agreement would smooth its path into Europe, but on 13 January 1963, Charles de Gaulle effectively slammed the door in Britain's face, citing its refusal to accept the European Economic Community 'without reserve' as his reason. However, de Gaulle ameliorated his rebuff to Britain's membership of the EEC by emphasising 'that nothing would prevent the close relationship and direct co-operation, as these two countries have proved, by deciding to build together the supersonic aircraft Concorde.'

This was the first time the name Concorde was used publicly, although it had first been uttered by the son of BAC employee FG Clark, and agreed with the French. Much was later made of the spelling, with the British Government insisting for some years to drop the 'e', and BAC public information equally adamant to use the 'e', before common sense eventually prevailed.

This was a far from easy period. The organisation of two management teams, with the chairmanship alternating yearly between Sud-Aviation and BAC, was cumbersome and unwieldy, and slowed down the decision-making process. It was held together only through the mutual respect for each other by BAC chairman Sir George Edwards and General André Puget, the latter being the first chairman of the Airframe Committee. Development costs escalated from the £95 million originally estimated to eventually jump close to £1 billion. The new Labour Government, which came into power in 1964, wanted to kill off Concorde, but found that the 'no break' clause enshrined in the November 1962 agreement prevented it doing so without heavy penalties. The political and technical sparring went on unabated, but in the end, Concorde became a real aeroplane, and a potent symbol of European co-operation and technical achievement.

CONCORDE GROWS

The latest design, on the basis of which the Anglo-French agreement was signed, showed that both aircraft would carry 100 passengers at a speed of Mach 2.2, the medium-range version over stage lengths of up to 2,400nm (4,400km), and the long-range version over stages of up to 3,250nm (6,000km). Maximum take-off weights were given as 220,500lb (100,000kg) and 262,500lb (119,000kg) respectively. The medium-range aircraft was to be provided with air brakes and a built-in ventral stair, and the long-range aircraft was to have 'a limited reheating system' on each engine. Another interesting statement with regards to pilot vision from the flightdeck insisted that 'no direct forward vision shall be provided for transonic and supersonic flight.' This was one area designers later had to give way on.

Work on both versions proceeded for nearly another two years, in spite of the obvious British dislike for the Super Caravelle, and the equally vehement French opposition to the long-range model. But in May 1964, Sud-Aviation reluctantly accepted BAC's position that only a transatlantic aircraft would make commercial sense, and the medium-range variant was dropped. The British finally got their way, but it had become clear that a larger aircraft was needed to carry a full payload across the Atlantic. As early as 1960, Russell estimated that an all-up weight of 385,000lb (175,000kg) would be required, and the aircraft gradually moved towards that figure, starting with a virtual re-design in 1964. The fuselage was lengthened by 14ft (4.25m) and the wing area increased by 15 percent, giving a gross weight of 367,000lb (166,500kg). A more powerful Olympus 593 engine was matched to the new size aircraft. Another 6ft½in (2m) was added to the fuselage a year later, and the cabin lengthened to accommodate up to 140 passengers. The Olympus engine was further improved to provide up to 40,000lb (178kN) thrust.

Other changes were incorporated, largely the result of data obtained from high- and low-speed research aircraft. The first of these was the largely stainless steel Bristol Type 188, powered by two de Havilland Gyron Junior DGJ.10 engines, which had been intended to demonstrate sustained flight at Mach 2, long enough to evaluate the steady-state kinetic heating effects on the structure. It first flew on 14 April 1961, followed by a second prototype on 29 April two years later. However, the excessively heavy fuel consumption severely curtailed flight time at full speed, which made it impossible to adequately explore the effects of prolonged kinetic heating. Consequently it contributed relatively little to the Concorde programme.

Bristol had more success with the Fairey FD2, sometime holder of the world speed record, which it converted into the Type 221 with a lengthened body and slender ogee wing — similar in shape to that proposed for Concorde, but without the camber. In its rebuilt form, the Type 221 made its first flight at Filton on 1 May 1964 and went on to provide valuable data on high speed handling. This was backed up by complementary low speed handling data gained by the slender delta Handley Page HP.115, powered by a single Bristol Siddeley Viper BSV.9 turbojet. The H.P.115 took to the air on 17 August 1961, and over the next four years made many flights in support of Concorde development.

WORKSHARE

Even before signing the treaty, BAC and Sud-Aviation had agreed in principle on the allocation of design, production and research facilities, and the responsibilities to be assigned to each partner, but it took many more meetings and much hard bargaining before a firm agreement was put in place. France took the larger share of the airframe work (60:40), with Britain (which had already been developing the Olympus turbojet) gaining more engine work. The final agreement enabled BAC and Sud-Aviation to assign the work among their factories, which were given full responsibility for the detailed design and/or manufacture of the components and sub-assemblies allocated. In Britain, the bulk of the airframe work was given to Weybridge, including design and manufacture of the rear fuselage, fin and rudder. Weybridge was also tasked with the manufacture of the forward fuselage including the nose, (designed at Filton). The mid-fuselage section was also designed at Filton, but built in France. The droop nose was designed and built by Marshalls at Hurn.

BAC also had design responsibility for a number of systems, including electrical, fuel, oxygen, engine instrumentation and control, fire protection, air-conditioning distribution and de-icing. Rolls-Royce, which had taken over from Bristol-Siddeley, continued to develop the Olympus engine, with SNECMA responsible for the nozzle, and BAC Filton for the air intake and engine bay. Four Sud-Aviation factories obtained airframe work in France, including St Martin in Toulouse, Marignane, Bouguenais and St Nazaire, with Dassault at Bourges being given responsibility for the outer wing. Hispano Suiza took the main landing gear and Messier the nose gear. France was also responsible for the hydraulics, flight controls, navigation, communications and air-conditioning supply. Two final assembly lines were set up, one in France and one in Britain, but there was no duplication at the sub-assembly stage.

Inevitably, there was some friction as each company had its own way of working which differed considerably in method and approach, especially on a national divide. But these were not sufficient to markedly slow down progress. Physical construction began in April 1965 when the first metal was cut for the two prototypes. Thereafter, progress was swift, with sub-assemblies starting in October, and the large centre fuselage/wing section being delivered to CEAT in Toulouse for static and thermal testing in March 1966. During the next month, just one year after the first metal cutting ceremony, final assembly of the French prototype 001 began in Toulouse, followed in August by the British prototype 002 at Filton.

Work on the engine proceeded in parallel. In November 1965, the Olympus 593B (Big) engine had ran at Bristol, and in June 1966, the complete Olympus 593 engine and variable geometry exhaust assembly had its first testbed run at Melun-Villaroche in France. This was followed three months later by testing in the high-altitude facility at the National Gas Turbine Establishment (NGTE) at Pyestock, England, and in April 1967 by the first complete test run in the high altitude chamber at Saclay, France.

Other significant milestones achieved in 1966/67 included the commissioning of the main flight simulator at Toulouse, the first flight of the Vulvan flying testbed with the Olympus, and the delivery to RAE Farnborough of a 70ft (21.33m) fuselage and nose section for fatigue testing. In February 1967, a full-scale interior mock-up at Filton was presented for the first time to customer airlines, which by summer had reached 16, making commitments for 67 aircraft. The French insisted on calling these orders, but BAC was equally adamant that they represented little more than intentions to order, and warned that the elation felt should not be overplayed.

Even at that late stage, the design evolution continued unabated. In May that year, the design was unveiled for the pre-production Concorde, which differed primarily in having a fuselage lengthened by 8½ft (2.59m) and a revised visor. The

ABOVE: Central fuselage and partial wing assembly being pushed out of hangar at Filton.

LEFT: The Vickers Vulcan bomber flight testing the Olympus 593 turbojet.

rollout of the first Concorde prototype 001 at Toulouse on 11 December 1967 provided ample proof of that. One niggling disagreement between Britain and France, which then Minister of Technology Anthony Wedgwood Benn described as the only disagreement during the years of co-operation, was also resolved. As of that day, the British Government finally accepted the French spelling of Concorde. Tony Benn later famously said: 'Concorde has an 'e' for excellence, England, Europe and *entente cordiale.*'

two-piece visor and periscope were replaced with a one-piece visor and a small 'step' in the windscreen, which gave better forward vision. The fuselage stretch was accommodated forward of the wing. Together with moving the bulkhead further aft, these changes enabled 128 passengers to be seated in a single-class arrangement. Cabin windows were slightly reduced to meet FAA requirements, and an additional passenger door was provided over the wing leading edge. All these modifications were incorporated on the British pre-production Concorde 01, which made its first flight from Filton on 17 December 1971.

Language and cultural difference, the inevitable frictions of separate management organisations and two distinct production lines, as well as a two month strike by Sud workers at Toulouse in early 1968, often made for a difficult working environment, but these obstacles were overcome at all levels. The ceremonial

AIRBORNE AT LAST

The second prototype 002 began its taxi trials at Filton on 20 August 1998 and was rolled out the next month. With rumours circulating from the Soviet Union that the flight of the Tu-144 was imminent, the race to get the first supersonic transport aircraft into the air was on. This ended in disappointment for the West, when Tass reported that the Tu-144 had indeed taken to the air at Zhukovsky on the last day of 1998, achieving what both Khrushchev and Brezhnev had instructed the Soviet industry to do . . . to beat Concorde into the air. It proved a false dawn for the Soviets, and Concorde was not far behind.

Spectators had already marvelled for weeks at the sleek white shape roaring down the runway at Toulouse on taxiing trials, checking everything from brakes to engines and controls.

SST COMMITMENTS

	CONCORDE	BOEING 2707
Aer Lingus	—	2
Air Canada	4	6
Air France	8	6
Air-India	2	2
Airlift International	—	1
Alitalia	—	6
American Airlines	6	6
BOAC	8	6
Braniff Airways	3	2
CP Air	—	3
Continental Air Lines	3	3
Delta Air Lines	—	3
Eastern Air Lines	6	6
EL AL	—	2
Iberia	—	3
Japan Air Lines	3	5
KLM	—	6
Lufthansa	3	3
Middle East Airlines	2	—
Northwest Airlines	—	6
Pakistan International	—	2
Pan American	8	15
Qantas	4	6
Sabena	2	—
Trans-American	—	1
TWA	6	12
United Air Lines	6	6
World Airways	—	3
TOTAL	**74**	**122**

ABOVE: Concorde fin assembly at Weybridge.

ABOVE RIGHT: Final assembly of forward fuselage for first Concorde prototype.

BELOW RIGHT: Production Concordes on the assembly line at Weybridge.

By the end of February 1969, the prototype 001 (F-WTSS) was ready for its first flight, but the weather threw a final frustrating spanner in the works. Even on 2 March, Toulouse-Blagnac airport was shrouded in early morning mist, filling the gathered dignitaries and pressmen with foreboding, nerves taut, as they awaited the culmination of more than a decade of hard work mixed in no small measure with hope.

By early afternoon the weather relented, and this time, as Concorde accelerated, shadowed by the Meteor NF.11 chase aircraft and the MS Paris photographic aircraft, it was for real. As the nosewheel rose from the ground and Concorde lifted into the air for the first time at 15:38 hours local time, the cheering could be heard over the deafening roar of the Olympus engines under full reheat. With nosewheel and undercarriage locked down for safety, Concorde cut an elegant path through the skies over southern France, before André Turcat and his crew of Jacques Guignard, Henri Perrier and Michel Rétif, brought her down firmly without perceptible flare after a 29-minute flight. The braking parachute had to be deployed because the tailwind had forced the aircraft further down the runway.

When Concorde had rolled to a halt, Henri Ziegler, president of Sud-Aviation, and Sir George Edwards of BAC went forward with Brian Trubshaw, who was to fly the British prototype, to offer their congratulations. The significance of the

historic moment they had all witnessed was not lost on any of the crowd gathered at the airfield. In that magic moment, all the trials and tribulations along the way were forgotten.

BOAC chairman Keith Granville described the flight as a 'soaring triumph for everyone involved in this spectacular aeroplane.' Full-page advertisements in British national newspapers by Pan American proclaiming 'Welcome to Tomorrow', was evidence that the enthusiasm for Concorde even made it across the Atlantic.

It fell to Brian Trubshaw to take Britain's prototype 002 (G-BSST) into the air five weeks later on 9 April. It almost did not happen as the reheat system at first failed on No.4 engine. But, after shutting the engine down, Trubshaw tried again. This time the reheat ignited and at 14:24 hours the aircraft soared effortlessly into the skies, accompanied by the Canberra chase aircraft, and watched by Henri Ziegler, André Turcat, Sir George Edwards, Tony Wedgwood Benn, and a mass of press and the curious.

Helicopters ferried the VIPs across the 50 miles to RAF Fairford to greet the aircraft as Trubshaw and co-pilot John Cochrane brought her in after a short 22-minute flight. The crew, which also included flight engineer Brian Watts (test observers M R Addeley, J C Allan and PA Holding were also on board) had one minor scare when both radar altimeters failed on approach.

For Sir George Edwards, the successful first flight of the British prototype was particularly sweet. 'This sort of event is better to look back on than to look forward to,' he told the assembled newsmen, 'I do not know of any way in which you could have had this flight five weeks after the first one, unless you had the resources of the two countries behind you. I hope my successors will sell hundreds of Concordes.'

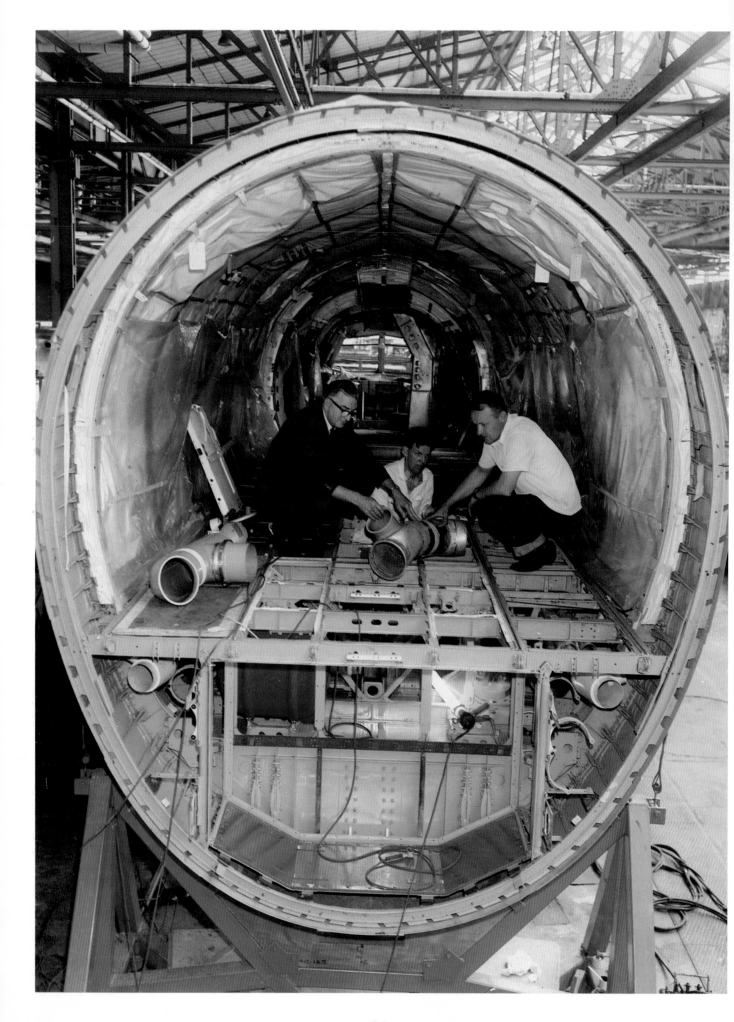

ABOVE: A dramatic night view of the second Concorde prototype.

RIGHT: Concorde 002 being prepared for ground engine trials.

LEFT: Air-conditioning being fitted to first production aircraft.

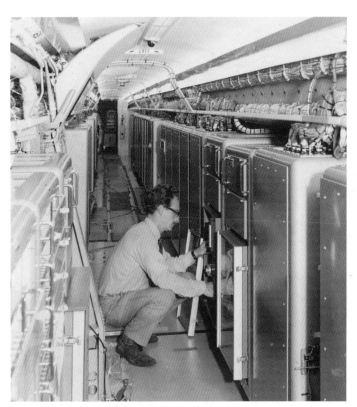

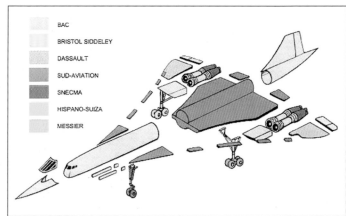

	BAC
	BRISTOL SIDDELEY
	DASSAULT
	SUD-AVIATION
	SNECMA
	HISPANO-SUIZA
	MESSIER

ABOVE: Concorde workshare distribution.

LEFT: Flight test instrumentation being installed on prototype 002 a few months before first flight.

BELOW: Positioning Concorde 01 fuselage in final assembly jig.

ABOVE RIGHT: Stewardesses from all the airlines that had commitments for Concorde line up for a special photo call at the roll-out of 001.

BELOW RIGHT: Concorde 002 lands at Fairford at the end of its maiden flight on 9 April 1968.

4 TESTING TIME

Concorde's first flight, while of momentous significance, marked only the beginning of a period when the aircraft would be put through its paces. Design calculations, computer analysis, wind tunnel results and simulator work could provide only some of the answers for an aircraft that touched the boundaries of contemporary knowledge, and sometimes crossed over into the unknown. In the end, only the bravery of test pilots could fully explore the performance envelope of Concorde and prove, or disprove, the ground-based assumptions during an extensive time in the air. There was little margin for error, and it was to the great credit of both designers and test pilots that the flight trials revealed no major problems and were completed successfully and without serious mishap. Numerous changes became necessary, however, to fine tune performance characteristics and ensure the safe and efficient operation of the aircraft in airline service. The consequent delay in the test programme is generally regarded to have been justified.

The overall philosophy of the Concorde flight development programme had been established in September 1964, when the British Aircraft Corporation (BAC) and Sud-Aviation agreed to split the programme into three distinct but overlapping phases, comprising development, certification and endurance flying. Development flying was essentially aimed at exploring the full flight envelope, identifying any inherent problems and providing feedback to the design teams for the implementation of corrective measures. The full flight envelope would again be explored in the certification programme, which by then will have incorporated any changes necessary to ensure the aircraft meets all requirements for a Certificate of Airworthiness (C of A). The third phase of endurance, more commonly known as route proving flights, was to approximate as closely as possible to actual airline operation.

The overall programme was agreed by January 1969, dividing the three phases into 1,935 hours for development, 795 hours for certification, and 1,500 hours for route proving, for a total of 4,230 hours, and utilising seven aircraft, including two prototypes, two pre-production machines, and three aircraft to full production standard.

The schedule planned for the first supersonic flight in summer 1969, Mach 2 by spring 1970, and airline service by the end of 1973. The first two came close, with 001 going supersonic on 1 October 1969 and Mach 2 being reached by the same aircraft on 4 November 1970, but the world had to wait until the beginning of 1976 before fare-paying passengers were allowed to fly on Concorde. But that had less to do with technical matters — although the many changes necessary inevitably impacted the schedule — and rather more with political and environmental issues, a lengthy decision-making process, and a generally hostile attitude, particularly in the UK.

The division of responsibility for the flight test programme reflected the general work split at BAC and Sud-Aviation, the latter becoming Aérospatiale on 1 January 1970, when Sud was merged with Nord Aviation and SEREB. As parallel production lines had been established for Concorde in France and the UK, so too were two flight test programmes. One was headed by André Turcat, vice-president flight tests at Sud-Aviation in Toulouse, and the other was led by Brian Trubshaw, general manager flight operations and chief commercial test pilot at BAC. The French took the lead on flying characteristics, while the British focused on performance.

As a result of in-flight evaluation and a continuous process of ground-based work, Concorde underwent many changes, with the result that there were major differences between the prototypes, pre-production and production machines. Concorde 01, which first flew on 17 December 1971, was a hybrid and not fully up to pre-production configuration. Predictably, the engine intake geometry took a great effort to solve, and flutter was also identified early on as an area of concern. On the positive side, supersonic drag assumptions proved over-pessimistic, with overall performance fractionally better than predicted, in spite of a slight increase of drag in the subsonic regime. The aircraft also proved much easier to fly than originally thought. A potentially difficult situation arose in the simulator during an engine loss at around Mach 1.7, which resulted in a change of the inner elevon gearing ratio, ie the movement in roll to the movement in pitch, from 1:1 to 0.2 on Concorde 002.

CONCORDE TEST PROGRAMME

A/c	Reg	First flt	1969 flt	1969 hr	1970 flt	1970 hr	1971 flt	1971 hr	1972 flt	1972 hr	1973 flt	1973 hr	1974 flt	1974 hr	1975 flt	1975 hr	Total flights	Total hours	Supersonic hours
001	F-WTSS	02/03/69	77	136h14	43	127h47	84	173h43	100	211h43	93	183h02					397	812h19	254h49
002	G-BSST	09/04/69	24	42h07	44	89h29	87	191h24	102	236h14	132	199h03	48	77h01			438	836h09	173h26
01	G-AXDN	17/12/71					2	2h07	83	197h19	51	116h23	95	231h03	39	83h12	269	633h10	217h03
02	F-WTSA	10/01/73									104	291h49	110	275h44	97	81h55	311	642h28	280h19
201	F-WTSB	06/12/73									3	10h06	108	273h17	261	526h17	372	809h40	297h16
202	G-BBDG	13/02/74											148	356h38	205	420h35	353	777h13	220h00
203	F-WTSC	31/01/75													172	503h21	172	503h21	315h59
204	G-BOAC	27/02/75													177	522h06	177	526h06	254h19
TOTAL																	2,489	5,536h26	2,013h11

ABOVE: A fine study of the second prototype Concorde G-BSST in flight.

BELOW: Concorde on cold-weather trials at Fairbanks, Alaska.

engine air intakes, which was vital if the aircraft was to operate at economically acceptable levels at both supersonic and subsonic speeds, took up nearly 10 percent of the whole programme.

This was found to have been too conservative and production aircraft later flew with a ratio of 0.7:1. At the low-speed end, the test team had to develop a new stall protection system on the prototype, which provided effective control over the aircraft's high-angle sink rate. The system developed provided two warnings to the pilot. At an angle of attack of 17°, a 'stick shaker' came into play on the control column, and this became a more pulsating 'stick wobbler' at about 20°, which could not be ignored. In between, an auto-stabilisation system ensured increased stability.

But as previously mentioned, much the greatest effort was directed towards developing the intake geometry, and on studying the airframe response to flutter, a high-frequency oscillation of the structure under the interaction of aerodynamic and aeroelastic forces. Three flutter tests were derived to artificially induce vibrations in the aircraft structure, which were then recorded on magnetic tape for later evaluation. These included electrically driven exiters, mechanically induced 'stick jerks' to study the effects of a sudden movement of the flying control surfaces, and thirdly, small explosive devices known as 'bonkers' attached to the wing and detonated in flight. Much time was spent on these tests, especially in the transonic regime where the greatest danger was expected, but no problems were encountered. Developing a sensitive control system for the

BOOM ALLEY

Concern over the effects of the sonic boom on old buildings and other structures led to the setting up of a number of measuring stations along Britain's West Coast, and in September 1970, Concorde 002 made the first of 50 flights down what soon became known as 'boom alley'. The usual flight path was to head east from Fairford under the control of

ABOVE: British-built prototype in the hangar at Filton.

ABOVE RIGHT: Concorde prototype F-WTSA achieving Mach 2 for the first time in November 1970.

BELOW RIGHT: Concorde in BOAC markings at Heathrow, together with three Vickers VC 10s.

London Military ATC, then turn north up the east coast, accelerating all the time to achieve the planned Mach number as the aircraft turned over the top of Scotland. The maximum Mach number was then held all the way south down the west coast, before throttling back for landing. The boom runs indicated that the overpressure levels were low and far less damaging to structures than the vibrations from passing heavy traffic, but the government still had to deal with many complaints from local residents.

On 4 November Concorde 002 made its first attempt to achieve Mach 2, but this had to be abandoned because of a fire warning on number two engine, later traced to a hot gas leak. On the same day 001 was airborne at Toulouse, and the news of the British failure spurred Turcat on to try himself, and he duly reached Mach 2. A second attempt by 002 on 9 November, also had to be cut short because of an oil leak in number four engine, but on the 12th, the aircraft eventually reached Mach 2.02 over the east coast. But on reducing power, an enormous double engine surge occurred twice on the right hand side as the aircraft dipped its nose and the wake from the wing leading edge was ingested by the engines, causing Trubshaw to remark afterwards: 'I thought that World War III had broken out.' Engine surges continued to occur at high Mach numbers, but the problem was later overcome by a redesign of the leading edge, incorporating increased camber. The first engine shut-down at Mach 2 occurred on 7 December following a gearbox failure on number four engine.

The first 100 supersonic flights were logged in January 1971, but on 27th of that month a major incident occurred

when 001 was engaged in deliberate surge testing at Mach 2 to determine the engine handling boundaries. On flight 122 when number three reheat was cancelled, the engine oversped and surged, followed immediately by an interactive surge in number four, which caused failure of a front ramp drive coupling. The ramp broke free and caused severe damage to the intake before being blown out. Pieces of metal were ingested by the engine, which was shut down, later restarted and shut down again. Examination on the ground revealed very heavy engine damage. Every compressor blade was damaged, as were the HP turbine rotor and stator blades, and only the LP turbine was considered salvageable, attesting to the toughness of the Olympus engine.

001 was flying again remarkably quickly, and in May made the first intercontinental flight to Dakar in West Africa. A trouble-free demonstration tour of South America followed in September. In June 1972, 002 left Fairford for a 45,000 mile (72,500km) sales tour of 12 countries in the Middle East, Far East and Australia, supported by an RAF VC 10 for the technical staff, and a Belfast, which carried two spare engines and other equipment. Some minor FOD (foreign object damage) to the engines was the only problem encountered. Airline demonstrations were given at Mach 2 in July 1972, and

in August, the 100th flight at Mach 2 was logged. In June 1973, both 001 and 002 made several high altitude sampling flights in support of a series of international research programmes, to improve knowledge of the stratosphere.

Concorde prototype 001 retired from the test programme that year and was flown by André Turcat on 19 October from Toulouse to Le Bourget, where it took its deserved place at the Musée de l'Air. It had totalled just over 812 hours on 397 flights, of which 254 hours were flown at supersonic speeds.

Prototype 002 carried on for another few months, before it too was retired after 438 flights, totalling 836 hours in the air, 173 of these supersonic. It was later handed over to the Fleet Air Arm Museum at Yeovilton to be preserved for future generations. During its testing time, 002 suffered only one real scare, when during a display on Avon Day at Weston-super-Mare on 26 August 1974, the left main gear supports detached, forcing the crew into a difficult emergency landing, which was executed successfully and with great skill. The subsequent investigation established that the retraction strut had buckled when the gear was lowered during a steep turn, and this design deficiency was corrected with a strengthening of the landing gear. But the designers had not got it quite right. Disappointing performance results from flight tests indicated that improvements were needed in solving the vexing thrust/drag issue, with lengthy arguments between airframe and engine manufacturers adding to the programme time. In the end, both had to make improvements, which were brought together for the first time in Concorde 02, the second pre-

wing twist, which involved constructing completely new wingtip sections, and fundamental changes to the engine support system and to the nacelle structure. Once in service, some operating limits of the aircraft were extended, providing further improvements in performance. These included an increase in the maximum structural take-off weight from 400,000lb (181,000kg) to 408,000lb (185,070kg), a 1,985lb (900kg) increase in the maximum regulated take-off weight, 3,307lb (1,500kg) more fuel, and a boost to the subsonic cruise Mach number from 0.93 to 0.95, generating a 1.3 percent reduction in subsonic specific fuel consumption (SFC).

OLYMPUS ORIGINS AND DEVELOPMENT

The Olympus engine was the world's first twin-spool turbojet. This revolutionary engine design, incorporating a two-spool layout with mechanically independent compressors, each driven by a single turbine, was submitted by the Bristol Aeroplane Company to the Ministry of Supply in 1946. After authorising the production of six units, the Olympus was first started up in a Bristol test bed in 1950. Although physically similar to its modern supersonic descendant, this early version developed less than a quarter of the thrust of today's Olympus 593.

After starting flying on a Canberra in 1952, the Olympus soon demonstrated its development potential and, as the Mk 101 went into service at 11,000lb (49kN) thrust on a Avro Vulcan bomber in 1956. By 1960, the Olympus had been re-developed with five stages of low-pressure and seven stages of high-pressure compression to yield 17,000lb (75.6kN) in the Mk 201, which went into Vulcan service that same year. In 1961, a Mk 201-equipped Vulcan set up a world record for non-stop flying in 1961, completing the 11,500 miles (18,500km) from Britain to Australia in 20 hours. The 20,000lb (89kN) Mk 301, with an extra low-pressure compressor stage, entered service in 1963, and a 30,000lb (133.5kN) supersonic version with reheat, the Mk 320, first flew in the TSR-2 multi-role strike aircraft in September 1964.

In early 1965, almost unheralded, the Olympus exceeded Mach 1 during a routine flight, signifying its supersonic credentials. The cancellation of the TSR-2 later that year was a blow to Bristol and the British aircraft industry, but 5,700 hours of bench and flight testing had yielded invaluable information, which speeded the development of the Olympus engine for Concorde.

The Olympus engine had first been proposed by British Aircraft Corporation for the BAC 198 and BAC 223 supersonic transport proposals in 1960, while the Olympus was also intended to be used by Sud-Aviation in France for the Super Caravelle. SNECMA, the French aero-engine manufacturer

production aircraft, and quickly proved their worth when the aircraft took to the air for the first time on 10 January 1973. Drag was substantially reduced through modifications to the wingtip camber, leading edges, and the application of a new fuselage tail cone, which extended well aft of the rudder and added a further 11ft 4in (3.45m) to the length of the aircraft. At the same time, reheat on the Olympus engines was extended to cover the transonic acceleration phase, mass flow was increased by a small percentage, and the secondary nozzle was redesigned . . . twice. The imprecise knowledge of predicting structural flexibility of the wing in flight also resulted in a redesign of the

Top: Sir George Edwards with Brian Trubshaw and André Turcat after a flight on 002.

Left: Concorde at Johannesburg on a demonstration tour to South Africa.

Right: Brian Trubshaw and Rooy Radford preparing for take-off from Johannesburg during the South African tour.

had also been gathering experience in exhaust and reheat systems with the Atar turbojet, designed for the Mirage supersonic fighter. The pooling of resources was the natural outcome with Bristol Siddeley and SNECMA signing a formal agreement for co-operation on 28 November 1961.

The UK was given design leadership on the engine. Bristol took responsibility for engine development and manufacture, while SNECMA tackled the complex reheat and variable geometry exhausts systems, to achieve a balance between fuel economy, low noise, and trouble-free service at the extreme temperatures of reheated operation. Bristol set about the design for a compressor system capable of operating at the high temperatures of supersonic flight, and later also devised a then remarkable electronic control system, which considerably improved engine performance in supersonic conditions.

The initial design for Concorde aimed for a 20 percent increase in the mass flow of air through the engine, compared with previous Olympus versions. The 12:1 pressure ratio of the -320 was retained by removing a stage from the rear of the high-pressure compressor, and adding a zero stage to the front of the low-pressure compressor, resulting in the familiar 7HP/7LP layout of the present engine. Cooling of the turbine

and other modifications to enhance service life were also incorporated and produced the 593D version. Two 593Ds were built, the first of which yielded 28,100lb (125kN) on test in 1964, the highest dry thrust achieved by any turbojet at that date. Although already obsolete because a major redesign of Concorde in 1963 demanded a 12 percent thrust increase, the successful 593D test programme clearly demonstrated that commercial supersonic flight was within reach.

The specification of the redesigned engine was finalised on 1 January 1964. First known as the 593B — for big — it was slightly larger than the 593D, with about 2½in (63mm) added to the intake casing diameter, and 10in (254mm) to the length. The 593B became available in 1965 and soon generated 32,800lb (146kN) of dry thrust, boosted to 35,000lb (155.8kN) with the addition of limited (9 percent) reheat. To avoid confusion, the engine designation was simplified and was henceforth known as the Olympus 593.

The Olympus 593 went on to become the most tested engine in the world. A new Vulcan flying test bed (the first one had been destroyed in 1962) was recruited for the development programme and first flew under Olympus 593 power on 9 September 1966. Flight clearance for operation up to Mach

1.6 was given for the 593 in 1968, by which time reheated thrust of over 38,000lb (169kN) had been achieved in bench tests. Both prototypes were equipped with the -3B standard engine when taking off on their first flights in early 1969. The rated thrust then was 34,370lb (153kN), although the -3B had generated more than 40,000lb (178kN) on test for a limited run. The Vulcan flying test bed was required for other purposes and made its 219th and last flight with the Olympus engine on 21 July 1971, after completing 420 hours in the air.

A lighter fuel pumping system with greater combustion efficiency produced the 593-4 engines, which were used on the first pre-production Concorde (01) and considerably reduced smoke on take-off. SNECMA continued with the primary and

secondary nozzle designs, and also tackled the noise problem with the so-called 'spade' silencers. However, in spite of numerous analyses and ground tests which predicted excellent noise reductions, the 'spade' silencers proved ineffective when fitted to the aircraft and operating at take-off speed, a failure that has still never been fully explained.

Major modifications were carried out during 1970, resulting in the first production engine, the Mk 602. The original combustion chamber was replaced with an annular type, with 16 fuel nozzles that vaporised the fuel before burning and virtually eliminated take-off smoke. BAC made a film about the modification entitled *Concorde gives up Smoking*, which it hoped would put an end to earlier jibes of Smoking Joe. A

ABOVE: Concorde 01 pre-production aircraft during final assembly.

ABOVE LEFT: Concorde prototype takes off from Toulouse.

BELOW LEFT: Air France Concorde in front of the Clement Ader assembly hangar at Toulouse-Colomiers.

re-designed intake section with five support vanes (reduced from 17) and zero entry swirl blades increased the gas flow through the engine by another 5 percent, bringing further thrust increase. The exhaust system was also transformed into the TRA (thrust reverse aft) configuration, replacing the multiple-petal type secondary nozzle by a 'bucket-type' design, which also acted as a thrust reverser, making significant weight savings and also permitting nacelle/wing trailing edge integration.

The Mk 602 was shipped to Toulouse in April 1972 and fitted to pre-production Concorde 02, which made its first flight in January 1973. In August 01 returned to Filton to be brought up to full production standard, including the fitting of 602s. The Mk 602 was also fitted to the first two production aircraft (201 and 202). Yet more refinements were announced in 1973, and included significant changes to the engine control system, which produced improved climb and supersonic cruise performance. Known as the Olympus 593 Mk 610 (full designation 593 Mk 610-14-28), this final development has been fitted on all production Concordes from aircraft 203, which first flew in January 1975.

Later that year, the Olympus received its final certificate of airworthiness. More than 12,000 hours were completed by the Olympus engine on the wing, backed up by another 18,000 hours on the bench. In 1988, the Olympus 593 reached a total of more than half a million flying hours in Concorde, half of those flown at Mach 2, a figure which then exceeded the combined supersonic experience of all the world's air forces.

AIRLINES GET COLD FEET

The technical side was only one aspect of Concorde's difficult and lengthy path into airline service. Political wrangling, a generally hostile media, protectionism by the United States to set noise standards high enough to keep Concorde from its airspace, the potentially threatening bankruptcy of Rolls-Royce, and simple economics, all contributed to often turbulent confrontations, which continued in parallel with the testing programme.

The airline 'orders' were still in place, and pilots from Pan American, TWA, Air France and BOAC had made the first assessments of Concorde towards the end of 1969, flying the aircraft at speeds of up to Mach 1.2, later also taking it beyond twice the speed of sound. Much to the relief of the manufacturers, performance figures obtained from the many flights undertaken by the two prototypes in the summer of 1969 showed that performance figures turned out almost exactly as predicted, with only a tiny 1 percent margin of error. Even so,

airlines continued to have doubts about the economic viability of flying the aircraft alongside the new high capacity Boeing 747s and other wide-body aircraft due to come into service within two years.

But for the sales teams, the early results from the test flights provided great encouragement to crank the marketing machine into overdrive, with 200 sales worth around £2 billion set as an achievable target. With the sonic boom taking on ever greater significance, obtaining orders from the four trans-Atlantic carriers took on the highest priority. BOAC, which had been a supporter since joining the STAC in 1956, had begun to cool, estimating that each Concorde would lose the airline £2 million a year. Yet, it accepted that, as the national carrier, it would be forced to operate the aircraft, as would its counterpart in France. Difficult negotiations with the British Government followed, during which the airline tried to obtain some compensation for losses, as well as suggesting the idea of a 'stretched' Concorde, which BOAC considered economically more viable and could actually be operated profitably. In the end, BOAC got neither, but signed for five aircraft at a cost of £115 million each, including spares, on 28 July 1972. Air France contracted to buy four aircraft on the same day.

Four days before, after the return of Concorde 002 from an extensive sales tour of the Middle East, Far East and Australia, the Civil Aviation Administration of China (CAAC) had signed a preliminary purchase agreement with Aérospatiale in Paris for two Concordes. The CAAC signed for a third with BAC on 28 August. The flight by Britain's minister of aviation Michael Heseltine and the Shah of Iran during the same sales tour also appeared to have paid off, with Iran Air signing a preliminary agreement for two Concordes and an option for a third on 5 October.

It was now considered only a matter of time before Pan American and TWA had to follow suit, if they were not to be left at a competitive disadvantage across the Atlantic, but the

order never came. On 1 February 1973 news came through from New York that Pan American would not be ordering Concorde. TWA also cancelled its interest and the other US airlines were expected to follow. The future of Concorde was suddenly thrown into doubt again.

The mood at the morning's press conference matched the cold drizzle and grey London skies, but Sir George Edwards masked his bitter disappointment with pragmatism. 'What we have to do now, makers and governments together, is to approach this situation with common sense and without panic . . . we shall not regard this — as somebody described it — as a mortal blow. It is a hell of a setback. Anybody who has been in this business for as long as I have gets used to it, but you may learn to live with it.' While Sir George made no secret of the

TOP: Nose-to-nose: Concorde at Airbus roll-out at Toulouse in 1972.

ABOVE: Prince Philip flies in the Concorde 002 prototype.

LEFT: British Airways mechanics work on the Olympus engines.

difficulties in selling to the Americans, he was generous in accepting that these cancellations were due to the parlous financial state of the airlines. Across the Channel, the French were less magnanimous, putting the whole episode down to a US political plot. Nevertheless, Henri Ziegler shrugged off this reversal and threw down the gauntlet to the world. 'I remain convinced that Concorde is a good aircraft . . . and that commercial supersonic flight will be with us in two years,' he stated. In the end, he was out by one year, but was proved right in the long run.

There were strong political reasons to push ahead with the project. Britain had finally been permitted into the European Common Market, and Concorde had played a not insignificant role in its acceptance, after previous French vetoes. Cancellation, in spite of the huge cost overruns, was now unthinkable. Failure of the supersonic airliner would have decimated the British aircraft industry and would have created unacceptably high levels of unemployment — estimated at around 25,000 in some 700 companies involved in Concorde work. The picture was similar in France, and Anglo-French relations would also have been strained to the limit.

Furthermore, Europe's attempt to wrest back some of the US control over the commercial airliner market would have been still born, probably for decades to come. Yet, the anti-Concorde voices, somewhat stilled since the successful first flight, saw the US 'conspiracy' as an opportunity to renew their calls to halt what they saw as a massive waste of resources, which could have been better spent on hospitals, schools, roads and other social imperatives. The Concorde lobby also argued that the sonic boom would make life miserable for millions, just to satisfy a few wealthy travellers.

But, although airlines dropped out one by one, leaving only British Airways and Air France, the programme continued. Route proving flights were conducted jointly by Aérospatiale and Air France on production aircraft 203 over the North and South Atlantic, and by BAC and British Airways with 204, covering the North Atlantic and the Middle and Far East.

These two aircraft flew 755 hours of the 1,000 hour requirement, with the remainder undertaken with development aircraft. All flying was undertaken with passengers and full cabin service. The route-proving programme threw up one or two unexpected problems, especially when experiencing sudden temperature fluctuations at Mach 2, which required changes to the autopilot, to provide a more consistent response to altering conditions and dampen out the more violent reactions. Five engines had to be changed on 204 because of a combustion chamber fault, adding further delays to the test programme.

With route proving the prelude to commercial service, airlines had to start calculating the cost of a Concorde ticket, trying to balance the need of making a profit with what would be acceptable to the travelling public. In 1975, Air France, for example, proposed to charge 20 percent over the first class fare to South America, first class fare plus 10 percent across the North Atlantic, and the normal first class fare on the envisaged Paris–Tokyo run. But these surcharges later had to be revised upwards to nearer 30 percent above the first class fare.

The final hurdle to be overcome before commercial services could commence was the Certificate of Airworthiness (CofA), which, after the successful completion of the test programme, was granted by the French Secréteriat Général de l'Aviation Civile (SGAC) on 9 October 1975 and by the British Civil Aviation Authority (CAA) on 5 December that same year.

It had taken 13 difficult years since the signing of the joint Anglo-French agreement, but commercial supersonic transport had now become reality.

TOP: Pre-production Concorde 01 en route to Farnborough Air Show for demonstration flight in September 1974.

LEFT: Concorde 204 at Bahrain in August 1975.

TOP RIGHT: Last four production aircraft during final assembly.

BELOW RIGHT: Sir George Edwards proudly shows off Concorde's Certificate of Airworthiness in December 1975.

5 TECHNICAL SPECIFICATION

The technical summary for Concorde covers descriptions of its fuselage structure, power plant, fuel system, flightdeck and flight controls, electric, air conditioning and hydraulic systems, landing gear, cabin interiors, and protective systems and emergency equipment. Only two models were produced, one for Air France and the other for British Airways. Although there are variations in equipment suppliers between the two, the basic systems and equipment scope is the same for both models.

STRUCTURE

The pressurised fuselage is of mainly conventional aluminium alloy semi-monocoque construction of constant cross-section, with unpressurised nose and tail cones. The basic structure, comprising five major sections — nose, forward, intermediate, centre and rear — consists of skin panels supported by extruded stringers and fabricated hoop frames at approximately 21½in (0.55m) pitch. A single row of windows extends along each side of the pressurised cabin, comprising a pressure panel and outer thermal insulation panel, both made of two layers of toughened glass separated by plastic interleaves. Window surrounds are formed of integral skin-stringer panels machined from aluminium alloy planks. The structure is free to expand longitudinally, to minimise the thermal stresses induced by the temperature differentials between the fuselage skin and the longitudinal floor members.

The cantilever wing is of ogival slender delta planform and slightly anhedral, with varied camber. It is a multispar structure skinned with integral panels manufactured from pre-stretched aluminium alloy planks. Spars are continuous across the fuselage, with spars and associated frames built as single assemblies extending between the engine nacelles. The forward wing sections are built as separate components attached to each side of the fuselage. There are three elevons at the trailing edge of each wing, manufactured from steel. Easily removable panels, together with the use of light and latticed internal members, provide access to any structure or fuel tank area, even in the thinnest section of the wing. The fin is a multi-spar torsion box similar in construction to the wing, with attached dorsal fin, leading edge, rudder jack and rudder hinges. The rudder is a single spar light alloy structure, manufactured in two parts coupled together. There is no horizontal stabiliser.

On take-off and landing, the entire nose fairing forward of the windshield, including the visor, is dropped to improve pilot visibility. The visor, which also protects the windshield from kinetic heating, has large transparent panels providing a good field of vision around the flight path. When raised, the nose and visor give the aircraft a clean aerodynamic shape. In general, the up position is achieved with mechanical uplocks, while the down position of the visor is maintained by hydraulic pressure and mechanical springs, and of the nose by hydraulic pressure, aerodynamic loads and nose weight.

Each engine nacelle accommodates two engines and is divided into two structurally independent parts: air intakes and engine bays. An extension of the engine bays incorporates the secondary nozzles. Intakes are of aluminium alloy construction with steel leading-edges. The structure between the firewall and wing rear spar is mainly of steel honeycomb sandwich, with conventional steel structure aft of the rear spar. The intakes and engine bays are attached to the wing by flexible joints, which ensure complete sealing and continuity of form.

The aircraft has two passenger and four cabin service exterior doors, upper and lower baggage compartment doors, and several miscellaneous ground servicing doors. All doors are operated manually. Two outward opening doors in the left-hand side of the fuselage — one forward and the other midway along the passenger cabin — provide normal entry and exit for passengers and crew, and can be opened from both inside and outside the aircraft. Four outward opening doors, two in the right-hand side opposite the passenger doors, and two, one each side of the fuselage at the rear, provide access for servicing between flights. These too can be opened from the inside or outside. All doors

LEFT: Concorde taking off with full reheat of its Olympus engines.

CONCORDE SPECIFICATION

	PROTOTYPE	PRE-PRODUCTION	PRODUCTION
External dimensions			
Wingspan	83ft 10in (25.56m)	83ft 10in (25.56m)	83ft 10in (25.56m)
Length overall	184ft 4½in (56.20m)	194ft (59.13m)	203ft 10in (62.13m)
Height overall	36ft 6in (11.10m)	38ft (11.58m)	40ft 1in (12.22m)
Max fuselage diameter	9ft 5½in (2.88m)	9ft 5½in (2.88m)	9ft 5½in (2.88m)
Wheel track	25ft 4in (7.72m)	25ft 4in (7.72m)	25ft 4in (7.72m)
Wheelbase	59ft 8½in (18.19m)	59ft 8½in (18.19m)	59ft 8½in (18.19m)
Internal dimensions			
Main cabin length	129ft 10in (39.57m)	129ft 10in (39.57m)	129ft 10in (39.57m)
Max cabin width	8 ft 7½ in (2.63m)	8ft 7½in (2.63m)	8ft 7½in (2.63m)
Max cabin height	6ft 5in (1.96 m)	6ft 5in (1.96m)	6ft 5in (1.96m)
Volume	8,440cu.ft (238.5 m³)	8,440cu.ft (238.5m³)	8,440cu ft (238.5m³)
Baggage/freight compartment			
Underfloor	310 cu.ft (8.78 m³)	227cu.ft (6.43m³)	227cu.ft (6.43m³)
Rear fuselage	265 cu.ft (7.50 m³)	470cu.ft (13.31m³)	470cu.ft (13.31m³)
Areas			
Wings, gross	3,860sq.ft (358.25 m²)	3,860sq.ft (358.25m²)	3,860sq.ft (358.25m²)
Elevons, total	344⅛sq.ft (32.00 m²)	344.5sq.ft (32.00m²)	344.5sq.ft (32.00m²)
Fin (less dorsal fin)	365sq.ft (33.91 m²)	365sq.ft (33.91m²)	365sq.ft (33.91m²)
Rudder	112sq.ft (10.40 m²)	112sq.ft (10.40m²)	112sq.ft (10.40m²)
Accommodation			
Passengers (typical/max)	100/138	100/148	100/131
Power plant			
4 x R-R (Bristol Siddeley)/SNECMA	Olympus 593-3B	Olympus 593-4	Olympus 593 Mk610-14-28
Thrust (each) without reheat	32,825lb (146.1kN)	32,520lb (11.7kN)	32,520lb (11.7kN)
Thrust (each) with reheat	34,370lb (153kN)	35,080lb (156.1kN)	38,050lb (169.3kN)
Weights and loadings			
Max ramp weight	412,000lb (186,880kg)		
Operating weight empty	135,610lb (61,510kg)	152,000lb (68,950kg)	173,500lb (78,900kg)
Max take-off weight	326,000lb (147,870kg)	350,000lb (158,760kg)	408,000lb (185,070kg)
Max landing weight	200,000lb (90,720kg)	218,000lb (98,885kg)	245,000lb (111,130kg)
Max zero-fuel weight	165,000lb (74,845kg)	183,000lb (83,010kg)	203,000lb (92,080kg)
Max design payload	26,000lb (11,795kg)	28,000lb (12,700kg)	29,000lb (13,155kg)
Max usable fuel weight	208,630lb (94.630kg)		
Performance			
Max cruising speed	Mach 2.2	Mach 2.2	Mach 2.2
Take-off speed	195kt (225mph/360 km/h)	195kt (225mph/360km/h)	214kt (246mph/397km/h)
Landing speed	162kt (186mph/300 km/h)	162kt (186mph/300km/h)	162kt (186mph/300km/h)
Rate of climb at S/L	5,000 ft/min (25.4m/s)	5,000ft/min (25.4m/s)	5,000ft/min (25.4m/s)
Service ceiling	65,000ft (19,800m)	60,000ft (18,300m)	60,000ft (18,300m)
Take-off field length	9,500ft (2,900m)	9,600ft (2,925m)	11,800ft (3,600m)
Landing field length	7,550ft (2,300m)	7,900ft (2,400m)	7,200ft (2,200m)
Range with max fuel	4,200nm (4,830ml/7,770km)	3,550nm (4,090ml/6,580km)	3,550nm (4,090ml/6,850km)
Range with max payload	3,390nm (3,900ml/6,275km)	3,390nm (3,900ml/6,275km)	3,360nm (3,870ml/6,230km)

can be used for emergency evacuation and are provided with escape equipment.

FLIGHTDECK

The flightdeck compartment on Concorde was designed to accommodate three operating crew members, plus an observer, with provision for a second observer's place. Oxygen and communication facilities are provided at each station. The captain's and first officer's position comprise a panel displaying flight instruments, and a centre panel containing engine instruments. Above the centre instrument panel is a glareshield containing autopilot, flight director auto throttle mode selection, as well as control for VOR/ILS frequency selection for each pilot. The left and right side consoles house the controls for nosewheel steering, weather radar and panel lighting.

The centre console provides mounting for the throttles and reverse thrust controls, together with visor and droop nose standby control, parking and emergency brake levers, standby landing gear lever, and communication and navigation control panels.

The roof panel is mounted centrally between the two pilots and is presented as a series of stepped sub-panels normal to the line of sight, and a flat panel to the rear of the sub-panels. The sub-panels contain master warning indications, switches for external lighting, controls and overheat warning lights for the de-icing and de-misting equipment, flying control inverter switches, autostabiliser, auto trim, artificial feel switches, and engine shutdown controls. The rear panel, accessible to all three crew members, comprises throttle system switches, HP valves, ignition controls, flying control hydraulic changeover, systems heater and anti-icing controls.

The systems management panels are located at the flight engineer's station, immediately aft of the first officer. It is arranged to enable the captain access to the more important switches when his seat is in the rearmost position. The panel layout comprises sub-sections presenting information on the power plant, fuel, hydraulics, electrics, air conditioning and pressurisation, oxygen, fire detection, and anti-icing systems. Where appropriate, panels are engraved with a logic diagram of the system.

Four seats are mounted on rails in the flight compartment, three of which, for the captain, first officer and flight engineer, are electrically operated, with the fourth observer seat wholly manual. A fifth seat, for a second observer, is stowed flat against the left-hand equipment rack. An electronically operated lock striking plate controlled by a switch on the flight compartment roof panel, provides the crew with an independent means of unlocking the flightdeck door.

FLIGHT CONTROLS, NAVIGATION AND COMMUNICATIONS

Concorde is controlled in pitch and roll by elevons, and in yaw by rudders. Each control surface is independently operated by a power flight control unit (PFCU), actuated by an electrohyraulic twin-ram servo control. The three elevons on each wing are arranged in two groups: the outer and middle elevons because their deflection angles are always synchronised, and the inner elevons, because their deflection angles in the roll axis are less. The control surface deflection angles are limited by mechanical stops. Lateral control reversal in the transonic region at high indicated airspeed, is avoided by a neutralisation system, which returns the outer elevons to the zero position at V_{MO} +25 knots. Conventional trim is provided in roll, yaw and pitch, with an electric trim system available only in pitch. The electric trim can be controlled either directly by the pilot using the pitch trim selector on each control column, or independently in auto trim when either autopilot is engaged or for automatic pitch stability correction.

The auto-stabilisation system improves the natural stability of the aircraft, through minimising the effects of turbulence and reducing the resulting flight path disturbance following an engine failure. The system generates independently supplied signals in pitch, roll and yaw as a function of aircraft rate of movement and Mach number from the air data computer (ADC), with no feedback to the pilot controls. It additionally provides a roll/yaw turn co-ordination function that reduces

Concorde also has an emergency flight control capability in pitch and roll axes in the event of a control jam between the control column and the relay jacks. There is no emergency flight control in yaw. Other high incidence protection is available via an incidence trim, which is part of the automatic pitch stability correction and operates at angles of attack of 11° and above, and a stick shaker on the captain's control column. Both columns will shake at an angle of attack of 16.5°, as the movement is transmitted to the first officer's control column through the mechanical linkage. The shaker is signalled from either ADC.

Each aircraft is equipped with an automatic flight control system (AFCS), designed to provide the capability for 'hands off' flight during climb, cruise and let down to a CAT III landing and, if required, a go-around. The AFCS comprises the following subsystems: auto throttle, autopilot, warning and landing display, and an interlock failure monitor and test system.

The auto throttle system provides thrust control of speed for approach and cruise flying, and also offers protection against overspeeds when the autopilot is engaged in the max cruise mode. Throttle reduction is initiated by the autopilot during an automatic landing. Instinctive disconnect switches on outboard throttle levers disengage the auto throttle, but as an ultimate safety measure, slip clutches allow direct manual override.

There are two separate channels each providing integrated autopilot and flight director systems. The autopilot signals operate in pitch, roll and yaw relay jacks in their autopilot mode and, via the mechanical control linkages displace the pilots controls. Normally both flight director channels are engaged, but both autopilots may only be engaged after land mode is selected. An autopilot instinctive disconnect button is placed on each handwheel, but the mechanical linkage between the relay jack and control column allows the pilot to overrride the autopilot commands.

The warning and landing display provides information on the operational status and functional capability of the automatic flight control system in its automatic approach and landing role, and displays autopilot and auto throttle warnings during cruise. There is also an altitude alert system, which provides audible and visual warnings of approach to and deviation from the altitude selected on the AFCS control panel. Although

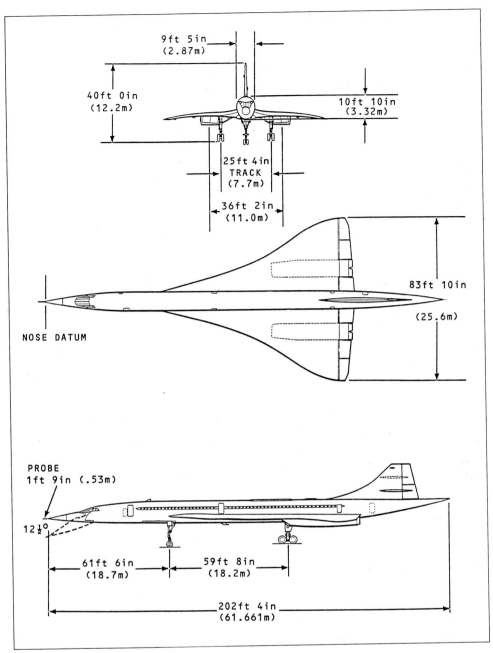

ABOVE: Concorde general arrangement.

ABOVE LEFT: Close-up of Concorde wingtip.

side-slip angles at slow speed in response to large lateral control demands. Artificial feel is provided on each control axis by a spring rod that increases the control stiffness with increasing control deflection, supplemented by dual control jacks, which change the stiffness as a function of speed, at speeds above approach speed.

The pitch artificial feel channels also provide the stick wobbler function of the anti-stall system. In addition to the stick wobbler, which creates an unmistakable warning through a pressure modulation in the artificial feel jacks causing both control columns to pulsate against any manual nose up force, the aircraft also has a second anti-stall system. The super-stabilisation function, which becomes active at angles of attack greater than 13.5°, produces a down elevon deflection through the pitch auto-stabilisation channel. The stick wobbler normally cuts in at an angle of attack of 19°.

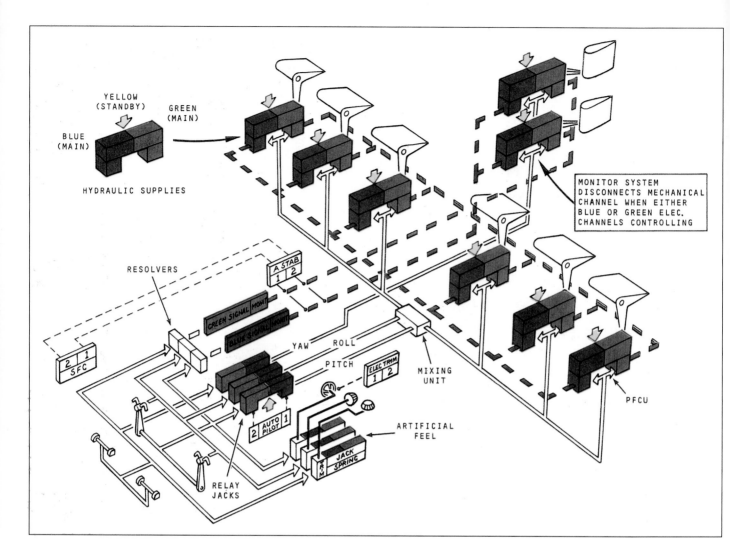

integrated with the autopilot/flight director, its function is independent of AFCS engagement states. Finally, the interlock failure monitor and test system continually surveys the engagement states of all the other systems that supply inflight data.

The navigation system includes both ground dependent and independent position indications, and has at its heart two air data systems supplied by two air data computers (ADC), located on the left and right hand sides of the droop nose. Each ADC has a built-in servo monitor system, which checks the servo channel operation for altitude, airspeed, Mach number, temperature, vertical speed and incidence. Three separate and independent inertial navigation systems (INS) provide navigation, heading and attitude information. Duplicated radio navigation systems provide bearings of a VOR or ADF beacon, distance to a DME beacon and localiser and glide slope indications, while the horizontal situation indicator displays commands from three sources, VOR, ILS and INS.

Two independent radio altimeters give low altitude information in the height range from 0 to 2,500ft (760m). Concorde is also equipped with weather radar, and a ground proximity warning system (GPWS), which issues visual and aural warnings. Basic communications comprise VHF and HF equipment, SELCAL, ATC transponder, and an interphone/PA system for flightdeck, cabin, galley, ground service and passenger address. A cockpit voice recorder is also installed.

POWER PLANT

Concorde is powered by four Rolls-Royce Snecma Olympus 593 turbojet engines with reheat, mounted in nacelles beneath the wings, each nacelle containing two propulsion units separated by a central firewall. Each propulsion unit comprises a variable-geometry engine air intake, the Olympus engine contained within an engine bay formed by the central wall, and a variable area secondary nozzle structure, which provides a mounting for the clamshell-type thrust reverser buckets forming the variable area secondary nozzle. The engine air intake is basically rectangular in cross section, with a moveable ramp in the roof and a spill door in the floor. Hydraulic actuators, supplied by the two main hydraulic systems, position the ramp to vary the intake capture area and open the spill door to augment the spill of unwanted air. At take-off and low speeds, an auxiliary inlet vane, integral with the spill door, provides extra air to the engine. A perforated bleed through the lower surface of the intake aids inlet performance at high Mach numbers.

The Olympus 593 Mk 610-28 is an axial-flow, two-spool turbojet with a take-off thrust of 38,000lb (169.1kN) including reheat. The basic configuration comprises a seven-stage LP compressor and seven-stage HP compressor, both manufactured largely from titanium, with the last four stages of the latter made from heat-resistant material, driven by single-stage LP and HP turbines. The annular combustion chamber is

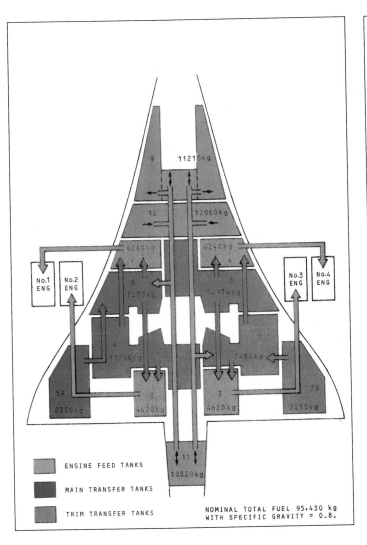

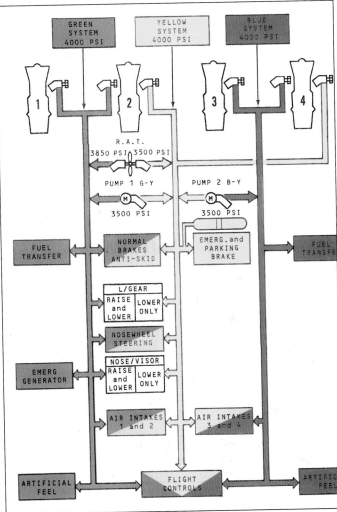

ABOVE: Fuel system tank location.

ABOVE RIGHT: Hydraulic power distribution.

TOP LEFT: Schematic layout of flight controls.

equipped with 16 vaporising burners, each with twin outlets, which leave virtually no visible smoke. Two gearboxes are attached beneath the compressor intermediate casing, both mechanically driven off the HP shaft. Combined control of fuel flow and primary nozzle area is achieved with the world's first FADEC (full authority digital engine control). Reheat fuel flow is controlled by an electrical unit.

The reheat system operates by burning fuel within the jet pipe, to increase the temperature of the exhaust gases, which increases the velocity and produces additional thrust. Reheat is normally used at take-off, and then switched off as part of the noise abatement procedure, and during the transonic acceleration up to Mach 1.7. Engines are started by low-pressure air acting on an air starter. Air may be supplied independently to each wing from a ground supply, or cross bled from the adjacent engine if it is already running. An auto ignition will normally operate in the event of an engine flame-out, but a manual relight facility is also provided. The variable area secondary nozzle is positioned fully open at speeds greater than Mach 1.1. At lower speeds, a nozzle angle scheduling unit

(NASU) positions the secondary nozzle as a function of the Mach number, and also provides the appropriate signals for the automatic selection of the engine control schedules. Protection against inadvertent reverser bucket movement is available. Reverse thrust is provided on all four engines for use on the ground, but may also be used in flight, but is limited to two engines, and only in reverse idle power.

FUEL SYSTEM

Fuel is stored in 13 sealed tanks, providing a total usable fuel capacity of 26,385Imp gal/31,605US gal (119,786 litres). The tanks are integral with the wing and fuselage structures and are arranged in three principal groups: engine feed, main transfer and trim transfer. This arrangement ensures that fuel is delivered to the engines at suitable flow rates, temperatures and pressures to satisfy all operating conditions. It also provides a means of controlling the aircraft's centre of gravity both prior to take-off and during flight, to match the differing aerodynamic pressure centres that occur during transonic acceleration and deceleration. Bugs on the CG indicators show the forward and rear boundaries of the CG corridor relative to Mach number. Because of Concorde's high climb rate, the fuel tanks are aerated to ensure that the fuel does not become a hazard.

Each engine has its own feed system from a collector tank, but a cross-feed system allows any engine or group of engines

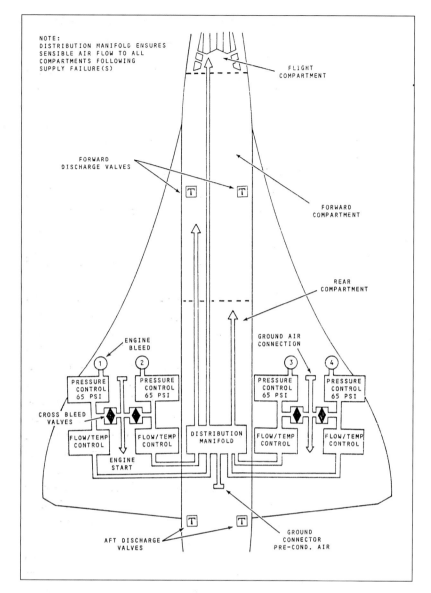

NOTE:
DISTRIBUTION MANIFOLD ENSURES
SENSIBLE AIR FLOW TO ALL
COMPARTMENTS FOLLOWING
SUPPLY FAILURE(S)

LEFT: Air-conditioning and pressurisation.

RIGHT: Electrical system schematic.

AIR CONDITIONING AND PRESSURISATION

The air conditioning system consists of four independent groups, each of which is supplied from an engine high-pressure compressor through a bleed valve, comprising a shut-off valve and a pressure-reducing valve. Four downstream cross-bleed valves allow cross feeding between two adjacent supplies on each side of the aircraft. Each cross-bleed valve also permits the ground supply of air from a high-pressure start truck for air conditioning purposes. In each group, the air passes through a primary ram-air heat exchanger to a cold air unit, and then through a secondary heat exchanger and a fuel/air heat exchanger. The primary and secondary heat exchanger cooling air is taken from an air intake on the engine nacelle at low speeds, and from a bleed inside the air intake at high speeds. Two jet pumps supplement the ram airflow when the landing gear is down. The fuel/air heat exchangers provide additional air cooling in supersonic flight.

Pre-conditioned air can be supplied directly to the distribution manifold through an external ground supply connection located at the rear of the fuselage. The four air conditioning groups supply air to a manifold, which distributes the air to the flightdeck and cabin. The equipment bay is cooled by fans, which extract the conditioned air from the cabin. The main landing gear bay is cooled by air bled from the cabin underfloor area, and also uses cabin air for ventilation, as does the hydraulic bay.

Cabin pressure is controlled and maintained by using discharge valves and a ground pressure relief valve to control the outflow of conditioned air from pressurised zones. Control includes two identical automatic systems, with limited manual control also possible. Cabin differential pressure is limited to 10.7 psi (0.74 bars) by the amplifier of the selected system, and to 11.2psi (0.77 bars) by the cabin pressure limiter of each discharge valve. The cabin altitude is limited to 11,000ft (3,350m) by a limiter on each discharge valve, and to 15,000ft (4,570m) by the discharge valve geometry, when all four air conditioning groups are operating.

ELECTRICAL POWER

Electrical power is supplied from four 60kVA engine-mounted integrated drive generators (IDG), giving 200/115V AC at 400Hz. During ground operations, power is supplied from an external source and can be connected to the aircraft distribution system through a single ground connection. Four 150A transformer rectifier units (TRU) are the primary source for the 28V

to be supplied from any collector tank. The collector tanks are replenished from the main transfer tanks 5, 6, 7 and 8 in a sequence that minimises the movement of the aircraft's centre of gravity. The trim transfer system is used to redistribute the fuel in trim tanks and main transfer tanks, so that the aircraft centre of gravity can be moved to optimum positions for take-off, subsonic and supersonic flight. The trim transfer is normally automatically sequenced and controlled from the flight engineer's panel, although a forward transfer override control is available to the pilots. The aft trim tank has four pumps, two of which are powered by their respective hydraulic systems. All tanks are vented, as well as being pressurised at high altitudes to facilitate pumping and preventing fuel boiling.

Fuel can be jettisoned through an outlet at the rear of the aircraft, with fuel supplied from two engine feed pumps in each collector tank. Refuelling is carried out through two refuel control units, located in the wing lower fairings forward of the main landing gear bays and connected to the trim transfer pipes. Selector switches allow simultaneous refuelling of all tanks, or individual tanks, for either partial or total filling. Refuelling can be carried out either automatically or manually.

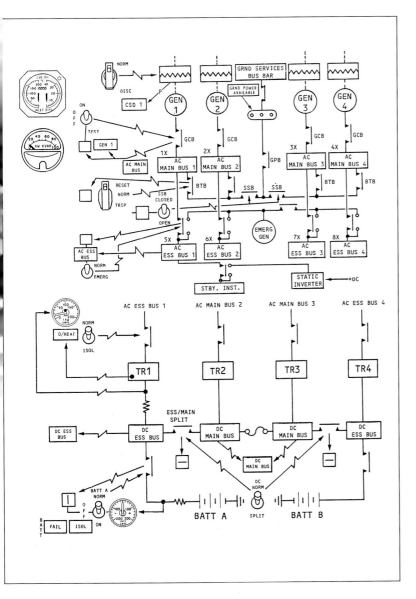

ram air turbine (RAT), a two-bladed propeller that cuts in to drive two hydraulic pumps in the event of the engine windmilling speed being insufficient to provide hydraulic and electrical power at subsonic speeds following a four-engine flame out. Ground generation is available by two electric pumps that can be selected to pressurise the main and standby systems while the aircraft is on the ground.

LANDING GEAR

The landing gear on Concorde is of conventional hydraulically actuated tricycle type, with two four-wheel tandem mounted bogies on the main unit, twin wheels on the nose gear, and a twin-wheel tail unit. A standby system, powered and actuated independently of the main system, plus a free fall capability, provide back-up. The main gear is fitted with dual, hydraulically-powered multi-disc wheel brakes with anti-skid control. An accumulator provides emergency braking pressure in the event of the loss of hydraulic systems. The main gear retracts inwards towards the fuselage centreline, while the nosewheel unit retracts forward. Normal operation of the landing gear is achieved through electrical control by the landing gear lever and the hydraulic system. Once retracted, hydraulic pressure holds the gear and doors. However, when the lever is at neutral, both electrical control and hydraulic supply are shut off, leaving the doors mechanically locked, so preventing inadvertent landing gear extension through control or actuator failure.

Free fall of the main landing gear is achieved through a mechanical device, situated under the rear cabin floor. If the gear does not lock down, pressurised air from the hydraulic reservoir pressurisation line can be directed to the telescopic side strut, which will extend the strut and engage the down lock, provided the gear is nearly down. The mechanical device for the free fall of the nose

DC supply, backed up by two 25Ah batteries. A hydraulically driven emergency generator is capable of supplying sufficient power for all essential electrical systems in flight. It starts automatically if any AC main busbar fails, or if No.1 and No.2 engines fail while airborne. On the ground, it will again start automatically if any AC busbar fails, but provided that No.1 or No.2 engine is above 58 percent N2.

HYDRAULIC SYSTEM

The hydraulic system actuates flying control units, artificial feel units, landing gear, wheel brakes, nosewheel steering, windscreen visor, nose cone droop, engine intakes, and fuel pumps in aft trim transfer tank. Hydraulic services are provided by three parallel, fully independent systems, including two primary systems and one standby, each powered by two engine-driven pumps. Each system includes a reservoir and is normally pressurised to 4,000psi (275 bars). In case of overpressure, a limiter allows a maximum pressure of 4,500psi (310 bars). An auxiliary air compressor is provided to ensure that the three reservoirs are pressurised before engine start, to prevent cavitation of the hydraulic pumps. Emergency power is supplied by a

Olympus 593 Leading Particulars	
Take-off thrust, including reheat (SLS)	38,000lb (169.1kN)
Cruise thrust (M 2.0 @ 50,000ft, ISA +5°)	10,030lb (44.6kN)
Specific fuel consumption (typical cruise M2.0)	1,190lb/lb/hr
	(33.71mg/Ns)
Pressure ratio (cruise)	11.3:1
Compressor stages	7LP + 7HP
Combustion system	Annular with
	vaporising burners
Turbine stages	1 LP + 1 HP
Overall length (flange-to-flange engine)	150in (3,810mm)
Maximum diameter	49in (1,220mm)
Intake case diameter	47½in (1,206mm)
Weight (dry engine) inc primary nozzle system	7,465lb (3,386kg)

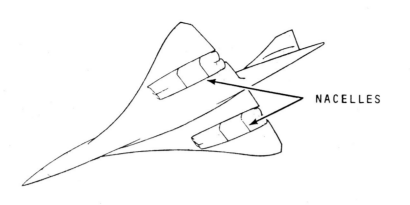

NACELLES

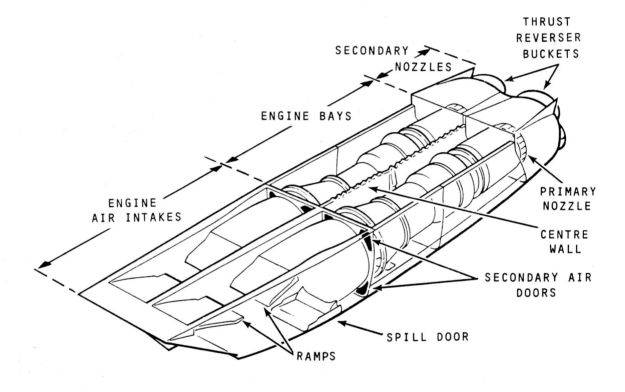

THRUST
REVERSER
BUCKETS

SECONDARY
NOZZLES

ENGINE BAYS

PRIMARY
NOZZLE

CENTRE
WALL

ENGINE
AIR INTAKES

SECONDARY AIR
DOORS

SPILL DOOR

RAMPS

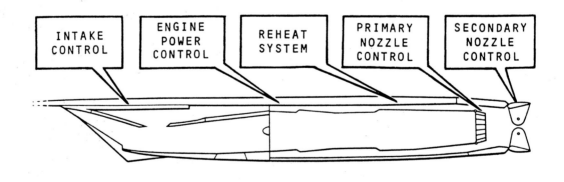

INTAKE
CONTROL

ENGINE
POWER
CONTROL

REHEAT
SYSTEM

PRIMARY
NOZZLE
CONTROL

SECONDARY
NOZZLE
CONTROL

ABOVE: General power plant arrangement.

OPPOSITE PAGE, TOP LEFT: Fuel transfer.

OPPOSITE PAGE, TOP RIGHT: Slide/raft deployment during emergency ditching.

BELOW RIGHT: Captain's dash panel.

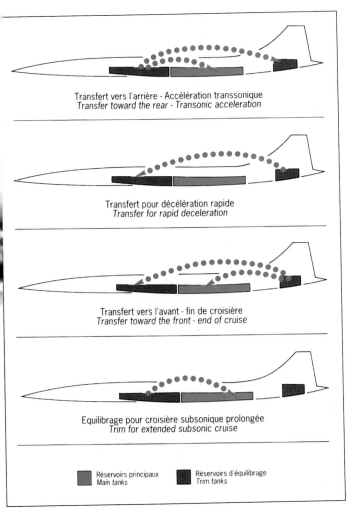

Transfert vers l'arrière - Accélération transsonique
Transfer toward the rear - Transonic acceleration

Transfert pour décélération rapide
Transfer for rapid deceleration

Transfert vers l'avant - fin de croisière
Transfer toward the front - end of cruise

Equilibrage pour croisière subsonique prolongée
Trim for extended subsonic cruise

Réservoirs principaux
Main tanks

Réservoirs d'équilibrage
Trim tanks

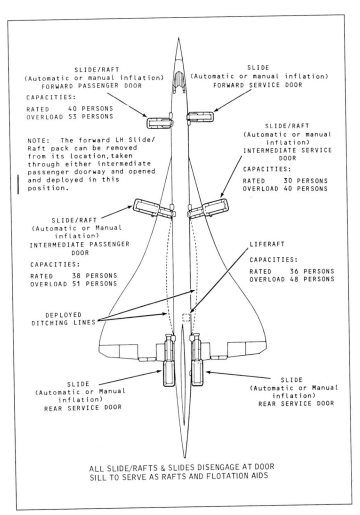

SLIDE/RAFT
(Automatic or manual inflation)
FORWARD PASSENGER DOOR
CAPACITIES:
RATED   40 PERSONS
OVERLOAD 53 PERSONS

NOTE: The forward LH Slide/
Raft pack can be removed
from its location, taken
through either intermediate
passenger doorway and opened
and deployed in this
position.

SLIDE/RAFT
(Automatic or Manual
inflation)
INTERMEDIATE PASSENGER
DOOR
CAPACITIES:
RATED   38 PERSONS
OVERLOAD 51 PERSONS

DEPLOYED
DITCHING LINES

SLIDE
(Automatic or Manual
inflation)
REAR SERVICE DOOR

SLIDE
(Automatic or manual inflation)
FORWARD SERVICE DOOR

SLIDE/RAFT
(Automatic or manual
inflation)
INTERMEDIATE SERVICE
DOOR
CAPACITIES:
RATED   30 PERSONS
OVERLOAD 40 PERSONS

LIFERAFT

CAPACITIES:
RATED   36 PERSONS
OVERLOAD 48 PERSONS

SLIDE
(Automatic or Manual
inflation)
REAR SERVICE DOOR

ALL SLIDE/RAFTS & SLIDES DISENGAGE AT DOOR
SILL TO SERVE AS RAFTS AND FLOTATION AIDS

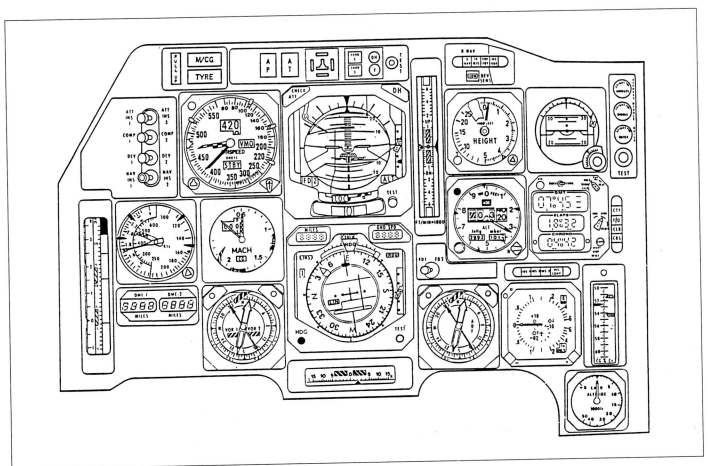

59

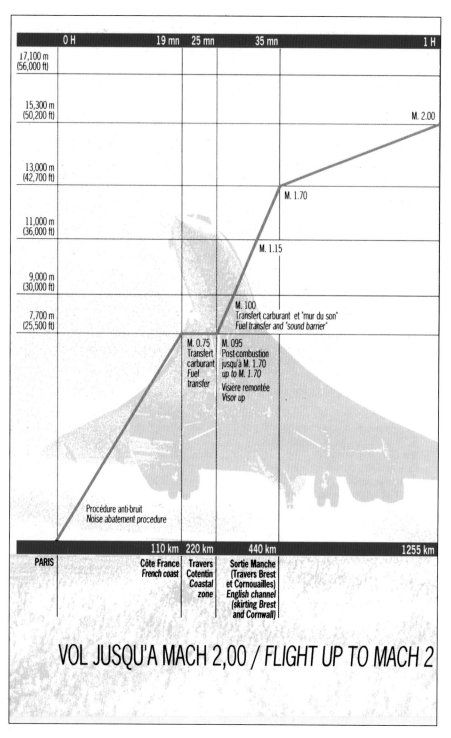

	0 H	19 mn	25 mn	35 mn	1 H
17,100 m (56,000 ft)					
15,300 m (50,200 ft)					M. 2.00
13,000 m (42,700 ft)				M. 1.70	
11,000 m (36,000 ft)				M. 1.15	
9,000 m (30,000 ft)					
7,700 m (25,500 ft)			M. 100 Transfert carburant et 'mur du son' Fuel transfer and 'sound barrier'		

M. 0.75 Transfert carburant Fuel transfer

M. 095 Post-combustion jusqu'à M. 1.70 up to M. 1.70 Visière remontée Visor up

Procédure anti-bruit
Noise abatement procedure

PARIS	110 km	220 km	440 km	1255 km
	Côte France French coast	Travers Cotentin Coastal zone	Sortie Manche (Travers Brest et Cornouailles) English channel (skirting Brest and Cornwall)	

VOL JUSQU'A MACH 2,00 / FLIGHT UP TO MACH 2

landing gear is situated under the forward cabin floor. Nosewheel steering is electronically controlled through the rudder pedals and hand wheels, and hydraulically operated.

INTERIORS AND BAGGAGE HOLDS

The cabin length of 115ft (35.04m) and width of 8ft 7in (2.63m) permits a wide variety of four-abreast layouts with a central isle width of 1ft 5in (0.43m) to suit individual airline requirements. Although typical layouts were marketed for 108 passengers in a superior class with 38in (0.96m) seat pitch, 128 economy class passengers with a pitch of 34in (0.86m), or a high-density 32in (0.81m) pitch arrangement for 144 passengers, both Air France and British Airways have limited seating capacity to 100 passengers. Both have also divided the cabin in two (40 and 60 passengers) with a bulkhead, to minimise the long tube effect. Two galley areas are provided, and toilet facilities are available at the front and centre. Baggage/freight space is available in two underfloor holds.

PROTECTIVE SYSTEMS AND EMERGENCY EQUIPMENT

The fire protection system provides detection through aural and visual indications, and extinction of a fire and/or overheat condition in the engine nacelles, together with smoke detection in the air-conditioning ducts and cabin and freight hold areas. The engine fire detection system consists of dual sensing loops, designed to warn of engine bay or torching flame type fires. Secondary air doors and engine bay vents, known as fire flaps, are closed to starve any fire of oxygen.

There is also a fuel tank vent ignition suppression system, which uses a flame detector to automatically trigger the discharge of an extinguishant into the vent pipe. This ensures that any external ignition of the vented fuel vapour cannot propagate back to the fuel tanks.

Simple temperature sensing elements monitor engine and nacelle overheating, while the wing overheat detection system consists of thermal switches in the rear equipment bay above each engine, to sense any leakage of hot air from the air conditioning system. Four fire extinguisher bottles, one in each engine dry bay, are electrically discharged from the flightdeck.

Concorde is also provided with two independent emergency low-pressure oxygen systems, one for the flight crew, and one for passengers and cabin crew, which employ gaseous oxygen from storage cylinders. In addition, portable cylinders are located on the flightdeck and in the cabin. A quick donning mask with diluted oxygen is supplied to each crew member on demand, up to an altitude of 32,000ft (9,750m). Above this altitude, the oxygen mask is supplied with undiluted oxygen at a progressively increasing pressure according to cabin altitude. A drop-down continuous flow system installed overhead and including oro-nasal masks is provided for passengers when the cabin altitude exceeds 14,000ft (4,260m).

An emergency evacuation alert system provides visual and aural warning for the flight crew and cabin staff. It consists of a bleeper warning and a flashing light in the flight compartment and in each of the cabins. The system is automatically actuated at all stations when the arming and control switch on the flight deck is set to the ON position.

Other emergency equipment distributed on the flightdeck and through the cabin includes fire extinguishers, radio beacons, a fire axe, battery-operated megaphones,torches, therapeutic portable oxygen bottles and masks, first aid kits, life jackets sufficient for passengers, crew and demonstration purposes, and flotation cots. Emergency egress from the aircraft is via cabin doors, but the flight crew also has the option of using the sliding windows, for which escape ropes are provided.

Escape slides are provided at each passenger door, with the forward and intermediate doors equipped with slide/raft combinations, configured to function as slides in a ground evacuation, and as rafts when detached from the aircraft following a ditching. A separate 36-person life raft equipped with rations and other survival kit is stowed at the rear of the aft cabin. An escape rope can also be attached to the doorway grab handle to permit a crew member to descend to the ground in an emergency evacuation when wind conditions limit the normal deployment of slides. Emergency lighting is provided for the passenger areas.

Ice and rain protection is provided for critical areas of the aircraft. The wing leading edges in front of the intakes and inboard to the fuselage, the engine intake and rear ramp leading edges, spill doors, and high speed air conditioning intakes, are de-iced by a combination of continuous and cyclic heating, while the engine inlet guide vanes are protected by hot air tapped from the engine.

Windshield and visor de-icing and demisting of the side windows on the flightdeck is accomplished by electric heaters, which have two temperature levels — HIGH and LOW. The visor heater operates only when the visor is locked up. Pressurisation static vents and drain masts are also electrically heated. The windshield wipers, deflectors and rain repellant systems are used in combination to ensure adequate visibility in all rain conditions. A wash system is used in conjunction with the wipers to clear the windshield of dust, insect or bird debris.

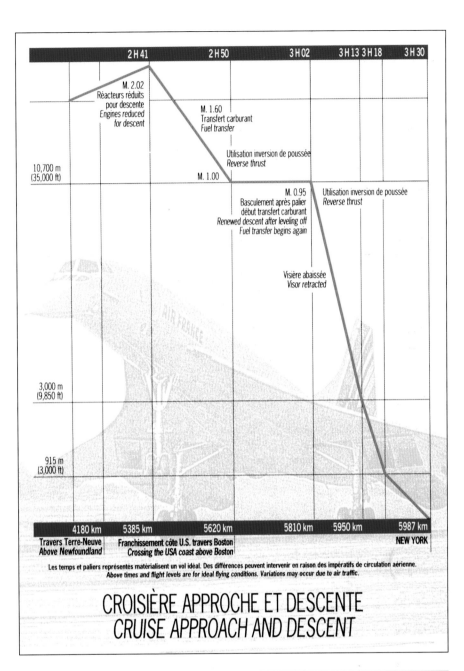

CROISIÈRE APPROCHE ET DESCENTE
CRUISE APPROACH AND DESCENT

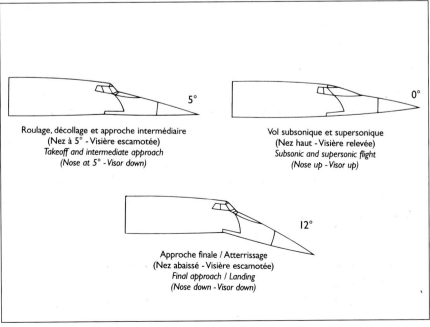

TOP RIGHT: Flight profile of Concorde service from Paris to New York (cruise approach and descent).

RIGHT: Nose and visor attitude in different phases of flight.

TOP LEFT: Flight profile of Concorde service from Paris to New York (up to Mach 2).

ABOVE: Flight engineer keeping an eye on the instruments during an engine test.

RIGHT: Flightdeck pedestal.

BELOW: Flightdeck roof panel.

TOP LEFT: Production Concorde flightdeck.

BELOW LEFT: Flightdeck of an Air France Concorde.

ABOVE: Flightdeck of an Air France Concorde.

LEFT: Twin-wheel nose landing gear.

BELOW: Variable-geometry engine air intakes on Olympus engine.

TOP RIGHT: Main landing gear with two four-wheel tandem bogies.

BELOW RIGHT: Olympus secondary nozzle structure with clamshell thrust reverser buckets.

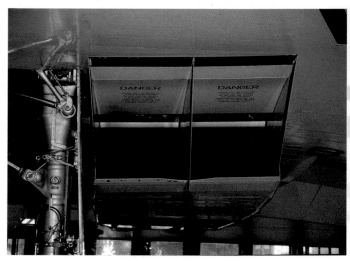

TOP: An Air France Concorde under engine test at Paris Charles de Gaulle.

ABOVE: One of the six Air France Concordes is always under maintenance.

LEFT: Close-up of Olympus engine air intakes and main undercarriage.

TOP RIGHT: Rolls-Royce/SNECMA Olympus 593 turbojet.

BELOW RIGHT: Olympus engine being worked on in the Air France maintenance hangar.

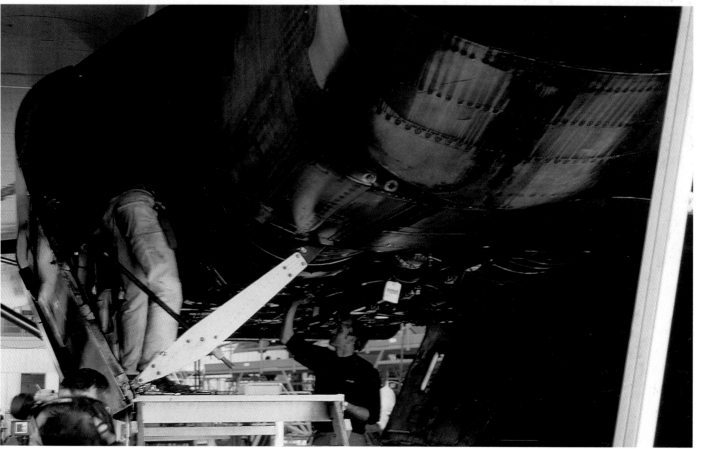

6 SUPERSONIC SOVIET

The whole truth about the development and subsequent short in service history of the Soviet Union's answer to Concorde, the Tupolev Tu-144 'Charger', is unlikely ever to be told. Rumour, speculation, disinformation, and not a little intrigue is what marked this rather striking supersonic aircraft and will continue to provide historians with countless hours in trying to solve a carefully constructed puzzle. What is certain is that in the Cold War era, the Soviet leadership was determined to beat Concorde into the air — whatever the cost. Prestige, rather than technological advancement *per se*, was the driver that was 'to grind the capitalists' noses in the dirt'.

After learning of the work being undertaken in Britain and France on Concorde, meetings were taking place in Moscow in 1962 between the Soviet Government and representatives of the aircraft industries, following which the Council of Ministers of the Supreme Soviet decided that it should be built at once. Its resolve was further strengthened when President Kennedy announced the US supersonic programme in June 1963, leading to the Presidium decision on 16 July to proceed immediately with the building of a supersonic transport aircraft for the national airline Aeroflot.

The order came down on 26 July to the Tupolev OKB from the then Soviet Premier Nikita Khrushchev, who regarded Andrei Nikolayevich Tupolev head and shoulders above other Soviet designers. Every effort was to be made to beat both

Concorde and the US aircraft into the air — failure to do so would not be tolerated. When Tupolev told Khrushchev at a Central Committee meeting that such an aircraft would be expensive to operate and extremely fuel-thirsty, Khrushchev told him that there was plenty of kerosene, but it was imperative that the world was shown that the Soviet Union was capable of building a supersonic airliner.

By that time, the Soviet Union had already started along the supersonic road by flying the Myasishchev M-50 'Bounder' four-engined heavy bomber on 18 October 1959. The appearance of the M-50 (also referred to as M-52 in some reports) during the Aviation Day flypast at Tushino Airfield in 1961, sparked off speculation in the West that the Soviets would be introducing a supersonic transport by 1965. Indeed, project studies on a SST are believed to have started around the same time under the designation M-53, which, as early as 1961, was apparently used as the basis for a performance specification drawn up by Aeroflot.

The rationale behind this early requirement can be found in the vast internal distances in the Soviet Union. It was calculated that a supersonic transport could provide a saving of over 36 hours compared to the fastest surface transport method. The emphasis was strongly on travel between Moscow and resources-rich Siberia, with the bulk of flights made up from bureaucrats, army generals, doctors and scientists. The SST

was clearly not intended for the masses, nor were international flights on the agenda at that time. Aeroflot was said to require a total of 75 aircraft to fulfil its state obligations. Even after the Myasishchev OKB was closed down by Krushchev, Vladimir Mikhailovich Myasichchev continued to prepare designs for possible SSTs. A model of a SST from that early work was tested in the wind tunnel on 14 May 1962, but nothing was heard subsequently about that particular project, or any of the others that had been discussed among the many Soviet designers since the mid-1950s.

From a virtual standing start and a timeframe of around five years, therefore, A N Tupolev had to produce an aircraft that required the application of new and some untested technologies. The General Constructor's son, Alexei Andreyevich Tupolev was appointed chief designer with Yu N Kashtanov as chief engineer, while the Antonov OKB was given the manufacture of the wing. The engine bureau of N D Kuznetsov was chosen to develop a suitable engine, based on the NK-8 turbofan for

ABOVE: Andrei Tupolev greets Captain Eduard Elyan after the successful first flight. *Novosti*

LEFT: The Tupolev Tu-144 on its first flight accompanied by the Analog MiG. *TASS*

BELOW: The Tu-144 crew on the first flight comprised, from left to right, Eduard Elyan, Yu Silvestrov, Vladimir Benderov and Mikhail Kozlov. *TASS*

the Ilyushin IL-62 airliner. Two flying prototypes and a static test specimen were ordered early in 1964, and Mikoyan was tasked with building the Analog A-144 with a tailless delta wing scaled down to fit a MiG-21. Using a slender delta wing required a fundamental rethink in Soviet aircraft design, as TsAGI (Central Aerodynamics and Hydrodynamics Institute) had always been insisting on a separate tailplane. However, wind tunnel results eventually convinced TsAGI that it provided the only answer to the proposed speed in excess of Mach 2.

For Soviet aircraft builders, the SST presented a challenge greater than any previously faced. Allied to the impossibly accelerated timescale, it was hardly surprising then that the Soviets turned to industrial espionage to help them on their way. British, French and US discussions on SSTs were closely monitored by Soviet intelligence, ensuring a steady leak of design ideas to the East. At the end of a visit to Moscow in 1963 by British Minister of Aviation Julian Amery and industry leaders concerned that the Ilyushin IL-62 appeared little more than a copy of the Vickers VC-10, the delegation was shown a small model of the proposed Soviet SST. Amery and his team were 'absolutely staggered by its resemblance to Concorde,' and alerted the Concorde builders to the possibility of industrial espionage upon their return.

While it is possible only to guess at the extent of this, two publicised occurrences, both foiled by the French, serve to illustrate the Soviet determination not to fail. In one instance, the French police arrested the head of Aeroflot's Paris office in a café with a briefcase full of Concorde engineering drawings in his possession, while an attempt to bribe an airport worker to collect samples of Concorde tyre rubber from the Le Bourget runway, led to a rather clever French counter-plot. The Aérospatiale laboratories created a compound that had no application for tyre use, which must have had the Soviet engineers totally baffled for a while.

A similar sting was executed by Aérospatiale in the field of metallurgy. Bristol-Siddeley at Filton was targeted especially, since the design of the engines was the weak link in the Soviet SST development. Spurious visits were made to the company's offices by spies posing as diplomats, journalists and others, and senior technical personnel from Bristol-Siddeley were invited to

Moscow in the hope that some information could be gleaned in one-to-one discussions. There were many other tales, more or less believable, but there is little doubt that the Soviet espionage machine was in full swing.

The display at the Paris Air Show in June 1965 of a model of the Tu-144 with an ogival delta wing confirmed for many observers that the Soviets had indeed resorted to industrial espionage, and the aircraft was quickly dubbed the 'Konkordski'. However, the model showed very little concrete detail, and, although superficially resembling the Anglo-French Concorde, there were distinct differences. Its fuselage cross-section, for example, was semi-oval, and the engines were bunched together on the fuselage centreline, with the exhaust nozzles stopping short of the wing trailing edge. When the prototype was finally revealed, the Tu-144 proved different in most respects.

A swing-wing delta for a Mach 3 aircraft, as proposed for the US SST, was also considered for a time, but was soon discounted, because of the considerable additional research required, especially in the development of materials capable of withstanding the higher temperatures. It was never quite shelved, however, and at the 1981 Paris Air Show, the Soviets exhibited a model of a Mach 3 HST (Hypersonic Transport).

PROTOTYPE REVEALED

Outline specifications given at Paris asserted a cruising speed of Mach 2.35, a range of 4,040 miles (6,500km), sufficient to fly from Moscow to Khabarovsk, a gross weight of 286,600lb (130 tonnes), and a take-off run of 6,235ft (1,900m). The seating showed space for 121 passengers in two cabins, the forward cabin with four-abreast and the rear cabin with five-abreast seating. But the design remained in considerable flux, as other models seen in subsequent years, were all different.

When the prototype finally appeared in 1968, it was slightly larger than Concorde, and had an ogival wing with the leading edge 76° inboard and 57° outboard, sweeping round to a large curved tip. The wing surface was basically in one plane, with only a modest camber on the inboard leading edge. While the leading edge was fixed, the trailing edge on each wing was formed by four almost square elevons, each driven by two power units faired into the underside of the wing. The design ensured that failure of one of the three separate hydraulic systems or one actuator would be confined to only one elevon on each wing.

The rudder was also divided into two units, each driven by two power units in separate circuits, although the fairings in this case causing prominent blisters. The Tu-144 was the first fully-powered civil aircraft in the Soviet Union.

BELOW: Andrei Tupolev with Henri Ziegler, president of Aérospatiale and head of a French delegation visiting the Tu-144 production facilities at Voronezh in 1972. *TASS/P Barashev*

ABOVE: Model of Tu-144 being prepared for testing at the Central Aerodynamics and Hydrodynamic Institute (TsAGI) in Moscow. *TASS/S Preobrazhensky*

The slender fuselage was basically circular in cross-section, with a diameter of about 11ft 2in (3.4m), with 25 small windows on each side and two main doors on each side measuring 66 x 30in (1,680 x 762mm), and small emergency doors at rear. The aircraft carried a flight crew of three, with the nose cone arranged to pivot down by 12° to give the pilots a better view for take-off and landing. The interior width of the cabin was 10ft (3.05m), and the height 7ft 1in (2.16m) over the 86ft 11½in (26.5m) passenger section, providing accommodation for a maximum of 126 passengers in a mainly 3 + 2 configuration.

Facilities for baggage and cargo were provided on the same deck front and rear, with loading via ventral doors, or by mechanical conveyors over the wing. The principal material used in the construction of the Tu-144 was aluminium alloy, with titanium leading edges and titanium or steel used in the region of engines, landing gear rib and other highly-stressed or hot areas.

After studying nine different arrangements for the main landing gear, Tupolev settled on an unusual 12-wheel bogie (four small tyres on each of three fixed axles), primarily to allow the unit to fit into the very thin wing. Each main gear retracted forward, the reverse of the usual OKB practice, the bogie rotating by 180° to lie inverted in the wing just outboard of the engine box. The tall nose gear was almost identical to that of the large Tu-114 turboprop airliner, and retracted rearwards into a large ventral fairing beneath the pressurised fuselage and the engine ducts. Brakes were fitted to all 26 wheels, backed up by a braking parachute in the rear fuselage. The four Kuznetsov NK-144 afterburning turbofan engines were grouped in pairs, rather than the originally proposed single box of four, each generating a thrust of 28,600lb (127.3kN) boosted with full reheat to 38,580lb (171.7kN). Reheat was not used in cruise mode. Stated fuel capacity was 23,090US gal/19,275 Imp gal (87,500l) in integral tanks in the outer wing, leading edge inboard and bottom of fuselage. Trim tanks were fitted forward and in the fin to provide centre of gravity control. As a result of this modification being incorporated at a very late stage, the pipe to the fin trim tank had to be fitted externally on the prototype.

FIRST INTO THE AIR

By mid-1968, the Soviet propaganda machine went into overdrive. Roll-out of the Tu-144 was scheduled for October, with the first flight to take place before the end of the year. The flight test schedule was to be cut to a minimum, to enable the introduction of the first commercial flight in March 1970. This was to be a flight between Moscow and Osaka in Japan, for the opening of the Expo '70 World Fair. Negotiations were also apparently underway for services to India and Pakistan. In the general euphoria, fantasy took over from practicalities and reason. Even before the prototype had been formally unveiled, the Soviet Deputy Minister of Civil Aviation, M M Kulik, stated that designers were already at work on a second-generation SST to replace the Tu-144 from 1980.

In December, the Tu-144, filled with test instruments and upward ejection seats for the crew, was ready for its maiden flight, but the weather had other ideas. When the crew arrived at Zhukovsky outside Moscow on 20 December, the airfield was covered in snow, and there was heavy fog and low cloud, with no sign of the weather improving. The crew waited for ten days, until on 31 December, an aircraft specially equipped for fog dispersing was even brought to the airfield and managed to clear a small window in the weather. The crew, comprising test pilot Eduard Vaganovich Elyan as captain, assisted by Mikhail Kozlov as co-pilot, flight test director Vladimir V Benderov, and flight engineer Yu Selivestrov, were given one hour to start-up, taxi-out, take-off and land.

The Tu-144, registered CCCP68001, was pulled out of its hangar by a bright red ZIL-150 truck and to the end of the runway by a Tatra tractor. Waving, the crew climbed up a steep yellow ladder into the unpressurised interior of the prototype. The NK-144 engines soon fired up and the aircraft rolled down the snow-covered runway past the gathered crowds of excited onlookers. After a 25-second roll, a supersonic transport aircraft took to the air for the very first time. The Tu-144, accompanied by the A-144 'Analog', spent 38 uneventful minutes in the air, during which, according to Elyan, it handled superbly. But that first flight was intended primarily to convince the world of Soviet prowess in technological development, and achieved its main purpose of beating Concorde into the air. Concorde did not make its first flight until 2 March the following year. Whatever its detractors may have said then and say now, getting the Tu-144 into the air represented a superb achievement. The exultation of the Tupolevs — father and son — was there for all to see.

A second flight was made on 8 January 1969, and the test crew soon extended the flight envelope into the supersonic realm, reaching Mach 1 on 21 May 1969. On the same day one year later, the aircraft made its public debut at Moscow's Sheremetyevo Airport, during which it made two slow fly-pasts. But its international presentation had to wait another year. By the time the aircraft achieved twice the speed of sound at 53,500ft (16,300m) on 15 June 1970 with Elyan at the controls, the Tu-144 prototype had completed 45 test flights.

The highest speed reached was Mach 2.4, with the design cruising speed having been set at Mach 2.35 (1,550mph/2,500km/h). Apart from these major milestones, few details were made known of the test programme, other than periodic comments that the aircraft performed and handled superbly, as expected. Some work was carried out on the duplicated environmental system, and the installation of variable inlets,

inertial navigation system and an autopilot. Elyan later referred to several flights in difficult conditions. On one particular take-off, when almost all Moscow airfields were closed to weather, the complete flight, including the landing, were performed automatically.

The prototype had accumulated only a total of 150 test hours when it was flown to the Paris Air Show, but it was imperative for the Soviet Union to show the red flag. The aircraft stopped at Prague for a Congress of Communist Party chiefs, before landing at Paris on 29 May 1971. Two days before, and in spite of intense lobbying based on the threat of the Tu-144 in the world market, a final Senate vote had killed the last hope for the Mach 3 US SST. The supersonic field had, therefore, narrowed down to just two, and Paris provided the first opportunity to compare the Soviet and Anglo-French examples side-by-side. This first 'confrontation' resulted in a multitude of expert opinions, but the general consensus was that the two aircraft were similar in outline, but differed considerably in detail. It was also noted that the Tu-144 prototype was rather worn and the design needed a fair amount of refinement for efficient operation at both subsonic and supersonic speeds.

Persistent rumours that a second prototype, which probably made its first flight in 1971, suffered an accident were never confirmed, but no picture has ever been published. Given the usual Tupolev practice of flying two prototypes, it would have been surprising had the whole flight test programme over more than three years been undertaken by just one aircraft. It has been suggested that the same registration was painted on two aircraft, to avoid embarrassment if one crashed. In his book on the Soviet SST, Howard Moon, says that such a switching game would explain the otherwise 'miraculous recovery of a severely damaged prototype at Warsaw in 1971 while returning from the Paris Air Show.'

After leaving Paris on 8 June, the Tu-144 remained at East Berlin during the DDR's Party Congress, and on 17 June flew on to Warsaw, where it had to make an emergency landing after two engines failed 20 minutes before touchdown. Polish mechanics reported wide cracks in the engine mountings and housings, suggesting severe vibration. However, the prototype left for Moscow the next day apparently fully repaired and was photographed a day later, giving credence to the suggestion of a switch.

There were clearly several unspecified problems to be resolved, and Andrei Tupolev had hinted at Paris that after more testing, the final version would 'differ somewhat.' When the first production aircraft appeared in late 1972, it had been substantially redesigned. Among the more pronounced differences were the straight double-delta planform of the wing, and the application of retractable high-lift canard foreplanes pivoted to the top of the fuselage just aft of the flightdeck. These more sophisticated features appeared to have been adopted from work by Myasishchev, noted on an early sketch design. A new wing with a span increased by 3ft 9½in (1.15m) and an area of 4,715sq.ft (438m^2), compared to 4,532 sq.ft (421m^2), was formed from two straight lines with squared-off tips. It had a pronounced camber across the entire chord root to

LEFT: The Tu-144 at Tashkent after flying from Moscow in 110 minutes on 20 September 1972. *TASS/Y Chuprikov*

tip and a marked downward curvature at the trailing edge. The elevons were modified and extended right to the tip, with a revised control system. The wing structure was altered to include more titanium alloy, especially on movable surfaces, a more extensive honeycomb structure, and integrally stiffened skins with welding replacing much of the riveting.

The engine nacelles were completely redesigned and now resembled those of Concorde, with oblique rectangular inlets separated by a central splitter, and electrically de-iced inlets with variable upper/lower profile. Four improved variable nozzles were separated by the width of the fuselage and extended aft of the wing, instead of stopping well short of the trailing edge. No thrust reversers were fitted. The nose gear was even longer than on the prototype, and was repositioned 31½ft (9.6m) forward, retracting forwards into an unpressurised compartment within the forward fuselage. An even more substantial redesign was noted on the main gear, which had eight-wheel bogies (four tyres on each of two axles) retracting forwards and rotating by 90°, to lie in a narrow, thermally-insulated and cooled bay between the inlet engine ducts.

The length of the fuselage had also been increased by 20ft 8in (6.3m), providing 34 windows on each side and accommodation for 140 passengers, with greatly improved structure and new materials used in its construction. A hydraulically opened entry door on the left of the nose replaced the ejection seats, and the nose cone itself was redesigned with a larger glazed area. The increase in weight from 130 to 180 tonnes (397,000lb) was accounted for almost entirely by additional fuel, which increased capacity to 26,155Imp gal/31,330US gal (118,750l), and enabled the aircraft to reach its design range of 4,037 miles (6,500km). The design also incorporated a greater capability for rapid fuel transfer nose-to-tail, and a special additive had been added to stabilise the fuel at high temperatures.

But the most striking difference was the addition of the retractable canard foreplanes, which resulted in major aerodynamic improvements. Each 20ft (6.1m) span canard was almost rectangular, with a double leading edge slat and double-slotted trailing edge flap, swinging open forwards to zero sweep, but sharp anhedral. They were extended at every take-off and landing providing powerful lift at the nose that enabled elevons to deflect down instead of up to give greatly improved lift at low speeds, as well as improved low-speed handling and agility. Another advantage was a reduction in required field length.

SETBACK

Andrei Nikolayevich Tupolev, the grand old man of Soviet aircraft designers, died on 23 December 1972. He lived just long enough to see the refined Tu-144 enter mass production at Voronezh, although latest predictions that the aircraft would enter commercial service in 1973 would prove to have been wildly over-optimistic. During the visit of a French delegation in December 1972, eight production aircraft were seen at Voronezh in varying stages of completion. The first aircraft (CCCP-77101) had flown in August, and on 20 September made a high-speed flight from Moscow to Tashkent, covering the 1,850 mile (2,980km) distance at an average speed of 1,680mph (2,700km/h) and flying at a maximum altitude of 59,000ft (18,000m).

The first flight of CCCP-77102 followed soon after, but this aircraft was tragically lost during a demonstration flight at the Paris Air Show on 3 June 1973, when a violent pull-up manoeuvre led to a break-up of the aircraft in mid-air. All crew on board, including Kozlov and Benderov, together with eight people on the ground were killed. The crash was yet another setback for the Soviet SST programme.

According to Alexei Tupolev, only some equipment was updated as a result of the crash, and production of the Tu-144 continued unabated. During a visit by US aviation journalists to Voronezh soon after the crash, the Deputy Director of the Ministry of Aviation Production, Mikhail S Mikhailov stated that Aeroflot had placed an initial order for 30 Tu-144s to service an ambitious route development plan, with an eventual total of 75 predicted. Aeroflot's plan then envisaged beginning SST services in 1975, first from Moscow to Novosibirsk, Irkutsk and Khabarovsk, to support the growing oil and gas business, followed by connections from the three Siberian cities to Leningrad. Moscow was also to be linked with Tashkent and Alma-Ata. Services to Europe were to be added by 1978, with the United States, Singapore and Tokyo following at an unspecified later date. There was talk of flying between Moscow and New York in 3½ hours. But as the oil crisis hit the world in December 1973, Aeroflot, hitherto an enthusiastic supporter of the fuel-thirsty aircraft, began to cool, and the prospects for export sales for the Tu-144 also diminished.

Nevertheless, Aeroflot crews had already undergone some training in spring 1972 and route-proving flights began in May 1974 between Moscow and several destinations, including the longest stage to Vladivostok, via Tyumen. On 26 December, CCCP-77106 began regular cargo flights between Moscow and Alma-Ata, routinely flying the 2,025 miles (3,260km) in under two hours. Economically, the service turned out to be a failure, and the twice-weekly flights were cut back to once a week in June 1976 and cancelled altogether the following December. A series of 50 proving flights commenced on 22 February 1977 over the 3,900 mile (6,280km) route between Moscow and Khabarovsk. On all flights, the crew was made up of one pilot from the OKB and one from Aeroflot, with a similar split among the flight engineers.

The omission of the Tu-144 in Aeroflot's five-year plan 1976-1980 was telling, but the Soviets were determined not to lose face. Against the background of Concorde's growing international route network and the advent of the 60th Anniversary of the October Revolution, the certification programme of the Tu-144 was accelerated. A whole range of trials — on the ground, static and in flight — were carried out, with certification flights led by Eduard Vaganovich Elyan and GosNII GA (State Science and Technology Institute of Civil Aviation) test crews, including Vladislav Popov, Nikolai Yurskov and Mikhail Kuznetsov. In October 1977, the Tu-144 received a proper Certificate of Airworthiness for passenger flights, the first Soviet aircraft to obtain one. On 1 November 1977, some five years late, Aeroflot began commercial

ABOVE: A long curved tip and four large almost square elevons mark the Tu-144 wing. *TASS*

LEFT: Tu-144 cockpit.

supersonic passenger services between Moscow and Alma-Ata. The first flight, with CCCP77109, was captained by Boris Fyodorovich Kuznetsov and carried 80 selected passengers, including the first from the West to fly in the Tu-144. Their impressions were generally unfavourable, with excessive noise and cramped five-abreast seating top of the list of complaints. Although five of the next six flights were cancelled, with no reasons given, Aeroflot made a total of 102 flights between the two cities, many of which suffered various in-flight problems. On 23 May 1978, an improved Tu-144D crashed on a test flight and all supersonic aircraft were temporarily grounded pending an investigation. Although passengers and crew arrived at Moscow on 30 May for the next flight to Alma-Ata, the Tu-144 stayed on the ground. The scheduled service on the day of the crash turned out to have been the last passenger flight.

THE SECRETIVE TU-144D

Route proving flights and the first passenger services had confirmed that the Tu-144 could not meet its range guarantees without a considerably reduced payload, but the D (Dalniya — long-range) model with new variable-cycle engines was designed to correct this deficiency. By the time the Tu-144D made its first publicised flight on 23 June 1979 from Moscow to Khabarovsk in three hours 21 minutes with chief designer Alexei Tupolev on board, the aircraft had already been in flight testing for four-and-a-half years. The first flight (CCCP-77111) is believed to have taken place on 30 November 1974, although no information was made available on that flight, nor on its subsequent test programme.

Official statements emanating from the Soviet Union after the Khabarovsk flight suggested that the aircraft was '50 percent more economical in operation' and was 'ready for series production.' It was also said that the Tu-144D would meet international noise regulations.

Reports about the variable-cycle Koliesov engines had first surfaced in 1970, but were dismissed by Western experts as beyond the capability of the Soviets. The Koliesov RD-36-51A engines were said to have a thrust of 39,690lb (176.6kN) each, and 48,500lb (215.8kN) with reheat, but their fate remains a mystery. In spite of the claims of dramatically improved efficiency, the engines evidently did not measure up to the demands of Aeroflot. This did not, however, stop the Ministry of Aviation Industry boasting at the beginning of 1981 that testing on the Tu-144D was 'virtually complete', and that the SST would soon be back in service. Early in 1983, the Tu-144D was dropped from Aeroflot's flight plan, presumably marking the end of the freight-only flights to Khabarovsk, and the reported freight schedule from Moscow to Tashkent.

In a published account in the early 1990s, Elyan enthused over the Tu-144D's aerodynamic performance: 'The modified Tu-144D had an amazing characteristic. She would keep the selected pitch angle on approach without deviation. Over the threshold, she would drop her nose and touch down softly — all without any inputs, just the air cushion effect. On touch-down, one could simply push the column away and let the aeroplane do the rest. Indeed, this was a technique we were

developing.' He also recalled practising short-field landings and talked about the aircraft's exceptional stability and manoeuvrability. Pilots who flew her, he said, couldn't say anything negative about the Tu-144D. But time had moved on, and for the Soviet Union at least, the supersonic era was effectively over.

After the cessation of passenger flights, the Tu-144 continued to operate some mail and test flights and even garnered 14 world speed and altitude records with payloads of between five and 30 tonnes, but it was quietly allowed to slip into obscurity. However, on the occasion of the first Moscow Air Show at Zhukovsky in August/September 1992, Western journalists were able to get close up to the 'Charger', with several aircraft tucked behind the flight line of displayed types. It created considerable excitement, especially when it was revealed that three were still flying in support of studies of the ozone layer and atmospheric anomalies such as solar radiation and magnetic storms. The SSTs were also being used by future Buran crew members to practise landings.

As a follow-on from an agreement on aerospace co-operation between Presidents Clinton and Yeltsin in June 1993, the National Aeronautics and Space Administration (NASA) teamed with American and Russian aerospace companies in a joint international research programme as part of its High Speed Research Program (HSRP). The object was to develop technologies for a proposed future second-generation supersonic airliner in the US, but was also designed to help Russia with its own Tu-244 project, one of the reasons for Tupolev suggesting the use of the Tu-144 as a flying testbed. The NASA-led US projects team also included experts from airframe manufacturers Boeing and McDonnell Douglas, engine makers General Electric and Pratt & Whitney, and flightdeck partner Honeywell. Flight testing was in the hands of NASA Dryden Flight Research Center at Edwards AFB, California.

Centrepiece of the research programme was the Tupolev Tu-144LL (Letayushaya Laboratoriya — flying laboratory), a stored Tu-144D with low airframe hours, and suitably modified to meet NASA's requirements. Registered RA-77114 (construction number 08-2), the Tu-144D had made its last flight on 28 February 1990, at which time it had accumulated just 83 flying hours — 27 supersonic — on 47 flights. Among the many upgrades and modifications required to turn the aircraft into a flying laboratory were the replacement of the Koliesov variable-cycle engines with the Kuznetsov NK-321 augmented turbofan engines, originally produced for the Tu-160 'Blackjack' heavy bomber. The NK-321s generated more than 55,000lb (245kN) thrust each with full afterburner. A new digital data system (Damien PCM) was installed to collect airworthiness data and data from experiments, and the aircraft was covered with thermocouples, pressure sensors, microphones and skin friction gauges to measure the aerodynamic boundary layers.

TOP LEFT: Tu-144 cabin arrangement as depicted by Tupolev in a promotional brochure. The reality was far less luxurious.

TOP RIGHT: Public address system.

BELOW: Maintenance on undercarriage showing the 12 wheels on the prototype.

The Tu-144LL was rolled out at Zhukovsky on 17 March 1996 and the initial flight phase began in June 1996 and was concluded in February 1998 after 19 research flights. A shorter follow-on programme involving seven flights was begun in September 1998 and completed in April 1999. 50 experiments were initially proposed for the programme, of which eight were selected, including six flight and two ground (engine) tests. The flight experiments included studies of the temperature effect on the aircraft's exterior surface, internal structure, engine airflow and temperature, boundary-layer airflow, the wing's ground-effect characteristics, exterior and interior cabin noise levels, handling qualities in various flight profiles, and in-flight structural flexibility. Ground tests studied the effect of air inlet structures in eight different configurations on the quality of airflow entering the engine, and the effect on engine performance of the rapid positional changes of supersonic shock waves in the engine air inlet.

The follow-on testing was used for further study of the original six in-flight experiments with additional data acquisition and analysis instrumentation installed. On the first three of the seven second-phase flights, the Tu-144LL was under the control of American pilots, the first Westerners to fly the Tu-144. The pilots, Robert Rivers of NASA Langley Research Center at Hampton, Virginia, and Space Shuttle pilot Gordon Fullerton from NASA Dryden Flight Research Center, evaluated the flying characteristics of the aircraft up to Mach 2, and carried out an experiment to define in-flight wing deflections. The reason for the latter was the result of the pressure distribution test conducted during the first programme, which indicated that the wing deflection on the Tu-144 was greater than expected. American-supplied transducers and sensors were also installed to measure nose boom pressures, angle of attack and side-slip angles. All flights were conducted from Tupolev's facility at Zhukovsky. With NASA's subsequent abandonment of its HSR programme, a second-generation SST remains elusive.

TOP: The Tu-144LL shows off its double-delta wing as it makes a low-level pass over Zhukovsky. *NASA*

LEFT: C Gordon Fullerton was one of two NASA research pilots who evaluated the handling of the Tu-144LL. *NASA/Jim Ross*

TOP LEFT: The large retractable foreplanes enhance take-off and landing performance. *Air Portraits*

BELOW LEFT: Roll-out of Tu-144LL at Zhukovsky.

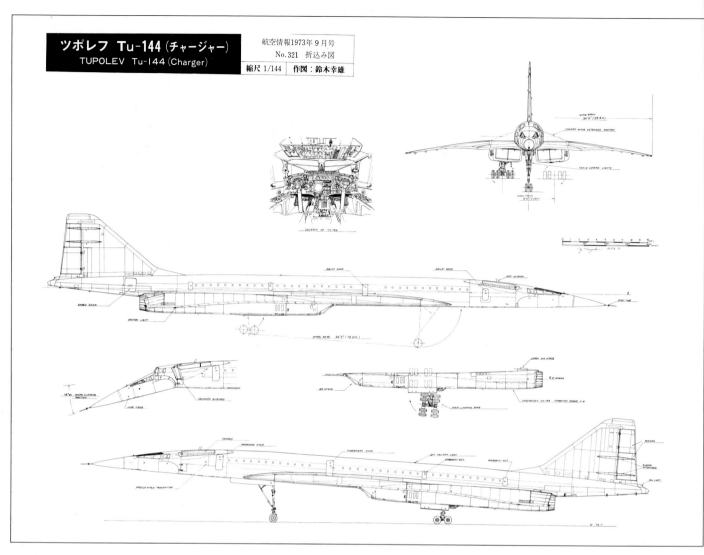

ツポレフ Tu-144（チャージャー）
TUPOLEV Tu-144 (Charger)

航空情報1973年 9 月号
No.321 折込み図

縮尺 1/144　作図：鈴木幸雄

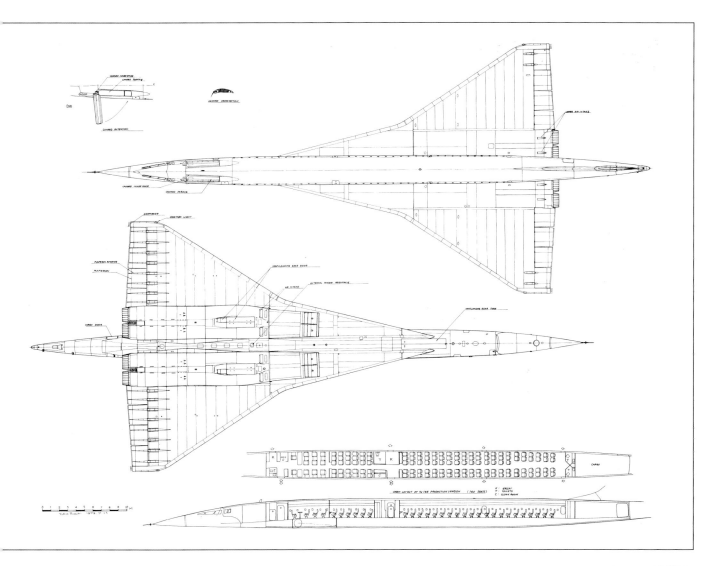

ABOVE LEFT AND RIGHT: Detailed drawings of production Tu-144. *via Aerospace*

LEFT: Graceful study of the Tu-144 just before touchdown. *TASS/B Korzin*

RIGHT: Almost a full passenger complement on the scheduled service to Alma-Ata. *TASS/B Korzin*

TUPOLEV TU-144 SPECIFICATION

	PROTOTYPE	PRODUCTION	TU-144D	TU-144LL
External dimensions				
Wingspan	90ft 8½in (27.65m)		94½ft (28.80m)	94ft 9½in (28.90m)
Length overall	194ft 10½in (59.40m)	215ft 6½in (65.70m)	219ft 11½in (67.05m)	
Height overall	42ft 2in (12.85m)		42ft 2in (12.85m)	41ft 4in (12.60m)
Max fuselage diameter	12ft 5½in (3.80m)	12ft 5½in (3.80m)	12ft 5½in (3.80m)	
Wheel track	19ft 10½in (6.05m)	19ft 10½in (6.05m)	6.05m (19ft 10½in)	19ft 10½in (6.05m)
Wheelbase	64ft 3½in (19.60m)	64ft 3½in (19.60m)	64ft 3½in (19.60m)	64ft 3½in (19.60m)
Internal dimensions				
Main cabin length	86ft 11in (26.50m)			
Max cabin width	10ft (3.05m)	11ft 9in (3.58m)		
Max cabin height	7ft 1in (2.16m)	6ft 4in (1.93m)		
Volume		5.763cu.ft (163.2m³)		
Baggage/freight		1,519cu.ft (43.0m³)		
Areas				
Wings, gross	4,532sq.ft (421.0m²)	4,714.5sq.ft (438m²)		5,457.3sq.ft (507m²)
Accommodation				
Passengers (max)	126	140	140	
Powerplant				
Number and type	4 x Kuznetsov NK-144	4 x Kuznetsov NK-144	4 x Koliesov RD-56-51A	4 x Kuznetsov NK-321-44
Thrust (each) w/t reheat	28,600lb (127.3kN)	28,860lb (127.5kN)	39,690lb (176.6kN)	55,077lb (245kN)
Thrust (each) with reheat	38,580lb (171.6kN)	44,090lb (196.1kN)	48.500lb (215.8kN)	
Weights and loadings				
Operating weight empty	174,165lb (79,000kg)	187,400lb (85,000kg)		216,050lb (98,000kg)
Max take-off weight	330,690lb (150,000kg)	396,830lb (180,000kg)	418,875lb (190,000kg)	456,350lb (207,000kg)
Max landing weight	264,550lb (120,000kg)			
Max zero-fuel weight	200,000lb (90,700kg)	220,460lb (100,000kg)		
Max payload			33,070lb (15,000kg)	
Max fuel weight	70,000kg (154,320lb)	209,440lb (95,000kg)		220,460lb (100,000kg)
Performance				
Max cruising speed	Mach 2.35	Mach 2.35	Mach 2.35	Mach 2.05
Take-off speed				
Landing speed		174mph (151kt/280km/h)		
Rate of climb at S/L		9,843ft/min (50m/s)		
Service ceiling	65,000ft (20,000m)	65,000ft (20,000m)	62,000ft (18,900m)	62,000ft (18,900m)
Take-off field length	7,550ft (2,300m)	9,845ft (3,000m)		
Landing field length	4,920ft (1,500m)	8,530ft (2,600m)		
Range with max fuel				
Range with max payload	1,730nm (1,900 miles/ 3,200km)	3,500 nm (6,500 km; 4,030 miles)	3,780nm (4,350 miles/ 7,000km)	2,973nm (3,417 miles/ 5,500km)

NB. These specifications are as complete as possible given the secrecy of the projects

TOP RIGHT: **Lift-off from runway at Zhukovsky on another high-speed research flight.** *NASA/Jim Ross*

BELOW RIGHT: **Tupolev Tu-144D is framed by the droop-nosed Tu-144LL.** *NASA/Jim Ross*

7 SILVER SERVICE

It may have been later than originally planned, but the long-awaited day had finally arrived. Millions of television viewers watched as the British Airways and Air France Concorde effortlessly soared into the skies, their take-off from London Heathrow and Paris Charles de Gaulle airports perfectly synchronised. The day was 21 January 1976 and the time 11:40 GMT. It was no ordinary day as the world witnessed the start of the first supersonic passenger services.

At 12:00 hours local time, passengers booked on Air France flight AF085 to Rio de Janeiro were requested to proceed to the boarding gate. Satellite 5 at Charles de Gaulle was crowded with passengers and some 600 guests of Air France. A hymn to Concorde was played on a nearby stage by a Brazilian orchestra, setting the scene for a pre-flight ceremony to mark this great occasion. Marcel Cavaillé, the French Secretary of State for Transport, accompanied by the ambassadors of Great Britain, Senegal and Brazil, as well as President Giscard d'Estaing and the president of Air France, Pierre Giraudet. The latter paid tribute to those who had worked tirelessly for 14 years to bring this great project to fruition. 'Many obstacles have been overcome thanks to the faith, perseverance and labours of all those who worked on Concorde,' he said, adding 'the technical challenge has been met successfully. We shall be equally successful in meeting the commercial challenge.' The British ambassador referred to 'a moment of triumph, made possible through unique, creative, exceptional and unprecedented collaboration between France and Great Britain.'

At the controls on that inaugural flight in Concorde F-BVFA were Pierre Chanoine as captain and Pierre Dudal as first officer. On board were 100 passengers, the oldest of whom, Mme Aurélie Ouille, aged 82, never missed an inaugural voyage. Concorde landed at 15:27 hours French time in the Senegalese capital Dakar, where the Senegalese president Leopold Sedar Senghor paid tribute to 'this triumph of technology.'

At 16:45 hours Concorde took off once more for its flight across the South Atlantic, landing in Rio de Janeiro at 16:05 local time (20:06 French time), delayed slightly by a minor problem in transitioning to supersonic flight after take-off. Nevertheless, the total journey time was only a fraction over seven hours, compared to the fastest non-stop subsonic flight of 11 hours and ten minutes.

TOP RIGHT: Splendid shot of six British Airways Concordes in formation. *British Airways*

BELOW RIGHT: The extension of British Airways' service from Bahrain to Singapore was flown jointly with Singapore Airlines, whose colour scheme was applied for a short time on the port side of the aircraft.

BELOW: British Airways Concorde takes off from London Heathrow on its first service bound for Bahrain. *British Airways*

The excitement was no less in London, as crowds, airport workers, journalists and VIPs gathered to witness history being made. In the cockpit of Concorde G-BOAA were Norman Todd as captain, Brian Calvert as first officer, and John Lidiard as senior engineer officer, with 100 passengers eagerly awaiting the take-off. Concorde streaked smoothly into the sky and landed at Bahrain at 15:20 GMT, after a 3,480 mile (5,600km) non-stop flight, covering the distance in 3hr 38min, as against the 6hr 15min required in a subsonic jet.

The two flights were marked by an exchange of good will messages from Her Majesty Queen Elizabeth II and French President Giscard d'Estaing. Her Majesty the Queen's message said: 'On the occasion of today's inaugural flights by Concorde aircraft of Air France and British Airways, I send you and the French people my warmest congratulations. Today's flights mark the successful outcome of 14 years of close collaboration between our two nations. It is a source of pride that our countries have today inaugurated a new era in civil aviation.'

Giscard d'Estaing's reply read: 'I should like in turn to pay warm tribute to the people and government of Britain, whose tenacity and talent were determining factors for the successful outcome of this great joint venture. Having shared its trials and tribulations for 14 years, today our two nations share pride in its success. I also share your pleasure, for in opening a new era in civil aviation, today's flights show what Anglo-French co-operation and friendship are capable of accomplishing for the benefit of scientific and technological progress.'

AMERICAN PIQUE

Rio de Janeiro, Caracas (Air France inaugurated a service to the Venezuelan capital via Santa Maria in the Azores on 9 April) and Bahrain were, of course, not the ideal destinations either

BELOW: Digital display in a British Airways Concorde indicating that the aircraft has reached the speed of sound at 29,000 feet.

OPPOSITE PAGE: British Airways Concorde G-BOAC taxiing at Washington Dulles after its scheduled service from London. *British Airways*

airline wanted to serve with its supersonic aircraft. Concorde was essentially designed around non-stop flights from Paris and London to New York, with Washington also on the shopping list. But the United States, still smarting from having been eclipsed by Europe's supersonic success, had other ideas. In summer 1974, the British and French governments had informed the US that the two airlines wanted to start services in early 1976, setting in train a process that was to lead to a prolonged and acrimonious battle.

The government approach was formalised in February the following year when Air France and British Airways officially sought approval from the Federal Aviation Administration (FAA) for two daily round trips to New York and one to Washington. In accordance with US law, an environmental impact statement (EIS) was published by the FAA on 13 November 1975, and followed by an announcement by William T Coleman, Secretary of Transportation, that arguments for and against Concorde could be aired at a public hearing on 5 January 1976. A decision was to be made a month later.

During the six-hour hearing, the speakers were divided almost equally on both sides. Those for Concorde on the US side included the deputy administrator of NASA, the director of supersonic develoment work at McDonnell Douglas and, interestingly, William Magruder, executive VP of Piedmont Aviation, who in the early 1970s as SST director at the Department of Transportation, had fought so valiantly for the continuation of the US SST. He now made a similarly impassioned, yet highly reasoned plea for Europe's SST.

Among the most vociferous opponents was the Environmental Protection Agency (EPA), which a year before had left it to the airport authorities to accept or ban Concorde operations, but now spoke strongly against. Its claim was that permission for Concorde would run counter to US policy on noise levels, the environment, and the quality of life. The EPA had a powerful ally in the State of New York, whose governor, Hugh Carey, had publicly announced that Concorde was not wanted at John F Kennedy Airport. A great deal of nonsense was espoused and written about the effect of Concorde on the environment.

American scientists got together to claim that if Concorde were to be allowed to land at New York, there would be 300 more cases of skin cancer, because of pollution and ozone depletion. Collapsing roofs, a weekly blow out of windows, and climate change, were among other preposterous stories put about. But it got sillier still, with one clergyman asserting that Concorde was a machine of the devil. That 'soap opera' had everything, except common sense, and showed America up for being small-minded and protectionist. Yet, much to his credit, Coleman carefully weighed up the arguments for and against and announced on 4 February that he would allow trial services into the US for

16 months, allowing 12 months of noise measurements and four months for analysis of results.

Coleman's fair decision represented a real breakthrough for Concorde, but the euphoria was tempered by the fact that the two airlines could not begin services to New York as planned on 10 April 1976. On 11 March, the Port Authority of New York and New Jersey had passed a resolution declining to participate in this demonstration, banning Concorde from JFK for at least six months, pending evaluation of operating experience at Dulles. The Coleman judgement did also not go down well with some powerful sections of the political establishment, leading to further bitter wrangling. But new President Jimmy Carter, who as presidential candidate had opposed US landing rights for Concorde, nevertheless upheld the decision.

Washington Dulles had never seen a day like 24 May 1976, when thousands of sightseers flocked to the airport to watch the almost simultaneous arrival of two Concordes of British Airways and Air France, inaugurating the first supersonic passenger services between Europe and the US. New Yorkers could board a Presidential Airways jet at LaGuardia Airport,

RIGHT: Air France advertising an additional service on its Paris–Washington–Mexico service.

BELOW: British Airways Concorde G-BOAB coming into land.

TOP RIGHT: An Air France Concorde landing at Auckland International Airport on a charter flight.

BELOW RIGHT: British Airways Concorde at London Gatwick.

specifically for the purpose of connecting to the Washington Concorde flights.

An intensive monitoring programme, involving the FAA, EPA and NASA, was set up at Dulles to obtain operational and public response data from the 16-month trial period, at the end of which a final decision on the aircraft's permanent access to the United States was to be made. The FAA monitored every Concorde approach and take-off, with results showing higher noise levels than subsonic jets at take-off, but quieter operation on landing. Overall, Concorde operated fully within the EIS parameters. There were numerous complaints from residents, but not excessively more than for subsonic jets, and were not always based on actual nuisance value. The FAA reported that some complaints were made on days when Concorde was not operating!

After six months, with decision time looming, the New York press took the opportunity to stir up public opinion further against Concorde by referring to FAA results at Washington, which appeared to show that Concorde would not meet the 112 decibel noise limit imposed at New York. Emotive headlines, such as 'SST flunking US noise tests', which appeared in the NY Sunday Times on 12 December 1976, were designed to whip up anti-Concorde feelings. It came as no surprise, therefore, when the Port Authority, which was due to make a decision on 10 March 1977, announced an indefinite postponement. The real battle for New York then began through the courts and spilled out into the political arena both at home and on a wider international level.

On 17 August, the Federal District Court ruled that the ban was illegal on the grounds that the Port Authority had been 'discriminatory, arbitrary and unreasonable.' New York State Governor Carey remained defiant to the end, but had eventually to cede, when the US Supreme Court refused to intervene in an earlier judgement by the appeals court that the ban was to end immediately. Even after services to Kennedy finally began on 22 November 1977, the port authority adopted noise rules designed to ban Concorde from 1985, but this never happened.

In the first 12 months of operations into New York, measurements of noise levels indicated that Concorde operated within EIS predictions. On 9 January 1979, again after a lengthy process, which had begun with the first informal talks in April 1961, Concorde was awarded its US type certificate by the FAA. This cleared the way for a subsonic 'interchange' extension of the Washington service to Dallas/Ft Worth by Braniff International Airways, which was inaugurated three days later. Braniff cockpit and cabin crew took over from British Airways and Air France crews on the domestic sector. The colourful US airline continued the service until 1 June 1980, when it was abandoned as uneconomic.

FAR EAST FAILURE

On 28 May 1976, the Australian Minister for Transport, Peter Nixon, had announced that 'the Commonwealth Government has given approval for the supersonic airliner, Concorde, to begin regular services to Australia.' His decision was based on noise and sonic boom measurements made during Concorde's

CONCORDE ROUTE	FASTEST TIME
London–Bahrain	4hr 10min
London–New York	2hr 59min
London–Washington	3hr 50min
Paris–Caracas	6hr 00min
Paris–Dakar	3hr 00min
Paris–Mexico City	8hr 00min
Paris–New York	3hr 45min
Paris–Rio de Janeiro	7hr 00min
Paris–Washington	3hr 55min

proving flights to Australia in August 1975 and a subsequent EIS, which, as far as noise was concerned, were similar to the results obtained by the FAA at Washington in the first days of Concorde operations. The EIS also stated that pollution of the atmosphere would be negligible, and that the audible impact of the sonic boom on the small number of people living under the supersonic path was likely to be no more intrusive than distant thunder.

British Airways was planning to begin services in February 1977, but the Concorde schedule never reached Australia. On 26 October 1977, British Airways and Singapore Airlines reached an agreement for an extension of the Bahrain service to Singapore, as the second leg towards Australia. The joint service was inaugurated on 9 December, but suspended after only three flights each way because Malaysia objected to Concorde flying over the Straits of Malacca. There followed year-long negotiations with the Malaysian Government, which eventually resulted in the resumption of the service on 24 January 1979. But overflight problems and poor loads continue to dog the service, leaving British Airways no choice but to cease operations on the entire route east on 1 November 1980. It had also wanted to fly to Tokyo and South Africa, but these were also never implemented. British Airways examined other possible routes, but could not identify any that would have improved the profitability of its Concorde operations.

Losses continued to mount, and were offset only by a successful and profitable New York run. The picture at Air France was very similar. In the first five years of scheduled service, the British Airways and Air France fleets, numbering seven aircraft each, had logged 15,800 flights, totalling over 50,000 hours, and carried 700,000 passengers.

Air France had added its third Latin American destination on 20 September 1978 by opening a service to Mexico City via Washington, and from 29 March 1981, implemented a change in its schedule, funnelling all of its 11 weekly North American flights through New York. Of this total, seven terminated in New York, while two others continued on to Washington Dulles and two more were routed to Mexico City. But the writing was already on the wall. The airline needed to cut the

ABOVE LEFT: Concorde promotional item.

ABOVE RIGHT: Close up of British Airways Concorde tailfin framing a Boeing 757 in the Chelsea Rose colour scheme, part of the airline's World Images identity. *British Airways*

RIGHT: Air France and British Airways Concordes side by side.

high operating cost of Concorde, and could no longer afford the heavy losses incurred on the South American services, forcing it to pull out of Rio de Janeiro and Caracas from 1 April 1982. Air France's supersonic routes to these cities had never attracted strong traffic, with average load factors staying under 50 percent. Even a special subsonic connecting flight for Concorde passengers at Rio aboard a VASP aircraft to Sao Paulo, failed to boost passenger loads. At the time of their closure, Air France was operating one flight a week to Caracas and two weekly roundtrips to Rio.

Worse was to come for the French flag-carrier. On 1 November that same year, it also had to discontinue its Washington and Mexico City services, leaving New York as its only Concorde terminus. British Airways on the other hand persevered with Washington, and even added a three times a week extension to Miami on 27 March 1984. But the British carrier also struggled to make money on these routes, first stopping the Miami extension in January 1991, before finally suspending its Washington route altogether on 1 November 1994. This was then replaced with regular charters to Barbados, which operated on a virtual scheduled basis. Interestingly, Sir Richard Branson was said at one time to have been interested in buying or leasing two Concordes for Virgin Atlantic's trans-Atlantic services, but nothing came of it.

MONEY MAKER

British Airways had realised early the possibilities of using Concorde on special charters, to provide the wider public with the opportunity to experience supersonic flight, as well as generate additional revenue to balance losses incurred on most of its schedules. Indeed, it was the charter business that has enabled British Airways to show a slight surplus on its Concorde operations. It began with one such flight in 1978, growing to four in 1979, seven in 1980 and more than 20 in 1981. Most of these were sightseeing flights over the Bay of Biscay, but there were also three to Cairo in Egypt.

The charter business grew substantially in subsequent years, largely through its preferred partner Goodwood Travel, whose Flights of Fantasy have carried 105,000 people on Concorde to 58 destinations, since its first charter to the Monaco Grand Prix in May 1983. Many notable charters on British Airways Concordes have included the world's first round-the-world by fare-paying passengers in October 1985, the biggest Concorde charter to one event when three aircraft flew to Nice for the Monaco GP in May 1988, the first Orient-Express trip from London to Istanbul with the return flight by Concorde in May 1990, and combined Concorde/QE II tours to Normandy for the 50th D-Day celebrations in June 1994. Goodwood Travel also organises the 1h 40m supersonic champagne flights over the Atlantic, and the annual visits to Father Christmas in Lapland.

Air France soon followed suit and has also built up a profitable charter sector, yearly carrying out some six round-the-world flights, several special promotions and incentive packages, and 20-25 champagne trips it calls 'flights to nowhere'. The last-named flights took off from Paris and head

CONCORDE FLEET DATA *(Active aircraft as of mid-2000)*			
Reg	Flying hrs	Landings	Supersonic
F-BTSC	11,816	4,817	3,559
F-BTSD	12,162	4,672	3,672
F-BVFA	17,214	6,741	5,276
F-BVFB	13,745	4,984	4,221
F-BVFC	13,398	4,555	4,083
F-BVFF	12,327	4,170	3,705
G-BOAA	22,769	7,394	6,842
G-BOAB	22,297	7,204	6,688
G-BOAC	21,531	7,016	6,543
G-BOAD	22,300	7,195	6,690
G-BOAE	22,380	7,342	6,707
G-BOAF	17,265	5,615	5,349
G-BOAG	15,088	4,976	4,729

into the Channel over Le Havre, before routing westwards and powering up to supersonic speed when well out into the Atlantic. After looping round off the west coast of Brittany, Concorde positions for the Channel Islands before landing back in Paris. Both the Air France and British Airways champagne flights take one hour and 40 minutes, sufficient to serve a three-course meal on board and, naturally, champagne.

Similar supersonic experience flights have also been made out of New York. Two of the more publicised special promotions using Air France Concordes were those by Pepsi and the US designer lingerie firm Victoria's Secret. For the former, Air France Concorde F-BTSD was rolled out on 2 April 1996 painted in Pepsi's blue colours to launch the company's new corporate identity. The Victoria's Secret incentive package involved a flight from New York-JFK to Nice on 14 May 2000, memorable for the presence on board of 20 of the world's top supermodels. The company's logo was more discretely applied to the top of the aircraft, although inside the cabin the pink headrests and menu cards provided a contrast to the normally classy and understated surroundings.

Of course, rich and famous people took their seats in Concorde every day, most on a regular basis. But there were also many notable VVIP flights, starting with Prince Philip who made a two-hour flight in 002 on 12 January 1970, followed on 8 May by HRH Princess Margaret, the Duke of Kent, Prince William of Gloucester and Lord Snowdon. On 7 May 1971, French President Georges Pompidou became the first head of state to fly in Concorde. On 26 June 1976, the UK Government chartered a British Airways Concorde for a summit meeting in Puerto Rico, and on 9 March following, the British Prime Minister James Callaghan used Concorde to fly to Washington. HM The Queen and Prince Philip returned from Barbados on Concorde on 2 November 1977, and again flew on Concorde to Kuwait on 12 February 1979 to start a three-week tour of the Middle East. There were, of course, many others, but should anyone believe that Concorde was and is only for the rich and famous, there have been many occasions where a much wider public had opportunities to ample the special Concorde service. British Airways has often surprised passengers by putting Concorde on normal domestic subsonic schedules, while Air France has given free rides even to its cleaners!

THE END FOR CONCORDE?

At the beginning of 1999, all those connected with Concorde experienced a feeling of déjà vu, as the United States once again threatened to ban Concorde from its skies. This rather drastic reaction was in response to a plan by the European Union to restrict hush-kitted aircraft two years ahead of the April 2002 ban on all Stage 2 aircraft. The US argued that the European unilateral anti-noise measure was a thinly veiled excuse for protectionism, since it largely affected US-built aircraft. Although the US House of Representatives voted by 412-2 to revoke the noise waiver that allowed Concorde to land at US airports, the threat was later withdrawn.

While there had been a few scares and publicised incidents in nearly 25 years of service, Concorde carried an unblemished safety record into the new millennium, a potent symbol of European technological achievement. But on 25 July 2000, the unthinkable happened. A chartered Air France Concorde, trailing a large plume of smoke and flames, came down near Paris two minutes after take-off from Charles de Gaulle Airport, killing all 109 people on board. Four more met their untimely end on the ground as the stricken aircraft ploughed into a small hotel in the nearby village of Gonesse. Air France

immediately suspended all Concorde flights pending the investigation into the causes of the crash. British Airways followed suit, although for one day only, with the Civil Aviation Authority (CAA) supporting the continuation of services by the British carrier. On the resumption of British Airways flights to New York, there was a high no-show, although there appeared no lasting reluctance by travellers wanting to fly on Concorde.

However, as the investigation began to establish that a tyre burst was the primary cause of the accident, British Airways was appraised of the findings and the intention to withdraw the aircraft's operating certificate on the morning of 15 August. British Airways immediately cancelled its morning flights to/from New York and ceased all supersonic operations that same day.

In a statement issued on 16 August, the CAA recommended that 'the Certificates of Airworthiness of Concorde be suspended until appropriate measures have been taken to ensure a satisfactory level of safety as far as tyre destruction is concerned.' A special exemption was made on 21 September to allow an Air France crew to fly Concorde F-BVFC, which had been left stranded at New York, back to Paris. Until that fateful day, more than 2.5 million passengers had flown on Concorde, in style, comfort and safety.

BELOW: **British Airways Concorde G-BOAF in the latest Union Flag colours.** *British Airways*

The joint manufacturers were to recommend an action plan to include appropriate measures to eliminate the risks associated with tyre bursts. This was followed by the setting up of a cross-Channel group to co-ordinate all efforts to find a permanent solution that would allow Concorde to fly again. Taking part in these discussions were the UK's Department of the Environment, Transport and the Regions (DETR) and the CAA, together with their French counterparts, the Ministere de l'Equipement des Transports et du Logement and the Direction de l'Aviation Civile (DGAC). Airframe and engine manufacturers, and airlines were invited as necessary.

These meetings, held roughly every fortnight, reviewed the results of the ongoing inquiry into the accident, as well as technical proposals submitted by the manufacturers to eliminate the presently unacceptable risks of tyre degradation and destruction. At the beginning of September 2000, the French Transport Minister confidently predicted that Concorde would fly again, and Air France chief executive Pierre-Henri Gourgeon even put a date to that possibility, suggesting that Concorde could be airborne again by May 2001. British Airways continued to plan for a re-introduction into service by April, backing up its confidence by proceeding with a £14 million refurbishing as part of its new strategy to concentrate on higher-priced premium services. The refit includes new interiors, as well as a new lounge at London Heathrow and glass piers at both Heathrow and New York JFK, to give passengers a better view of the aircraft.

There were many who predicted that the withdrawal of Concorde's certificate represented the end of supersonic passenger transport, possibly for 20 years. Indeed, the sight of British Airways' seven aircraft and the five remaining with Air France, standing forlornly on the ground, was a sad sight indeed. But in early 2001, both airlines began modifications that could allow Concorde back into service by autumn. These modifications include lining the wing fuel tanks with a Kevlar rubber lining, designed to contain the fuel if the tank is ruptured. The work package also includes additional protection for electrical and hydraulic systems, but there are no plans to make changes to the engines. Ground and flight testing was also started.

Looking further ahead, both Air France and British Airways had already implemented a life-extension programme to 8,500 reference flights (from the original 6,700), which would enable it to operate the aircraft until 2014. Air France, with lower utilisation had not reached the limit, but was also close to initiating a similar programme, having made a decision to continue flying Concorde until 2017.

Top: Needle-sharp Concorde noses its way into the hangar.

Right: Early Air France Concorde uniforms.

Top Right: A magnificent study of a Concorde taking off with full reheat of its engines providing extra thrust.

Below Right: Air France Concorde F-BVFA was the first to be delivered to the flag-carrier.

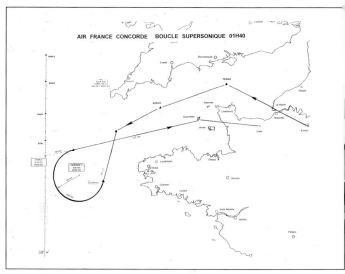

ABOVE LEFT: British Airways Concorde lounge at Heathrow. *British Airways*

ABOVE RIGHT: Air France boucle (loop) route for its Champagne charter flights.

LEFT: Air France Concorde logo.

BELOW: British Airways inflight service. *British Airways*

TOP RIGHT: Three magnificent British achievements: Concorde, the Red Arrows and the QEII. *British Airways*

BELOW RIGHT: Concorde painted in special colours during the 20-year anniversary celebrations at Toulouse in March 1989.

8 PAPER PROJECTS

The March 1971 decision by Congress to hold the US SST programme left the United States in something of a limbo, but it would have been surprising if all thoughts about supersonic transport had been abandoned. Consequently, technology studies into a future SST continued with the NASA Supersonic Cruise Research Program (SCR), originally known as the Advanced Supersonic Technology Program, albeit at a much lower level. The programme ran at an average annual funding level of US$10 million until March 1981.

In October 1976, NASA estimated the post-Concorde market to be 300 aircraft, costing US$90 million each, with US airlines taking half. Concurrently, the three major US manufacturers were also continuing studies, with Boeing looking at a blended wing-body with variable cycle engines, Douglas a less advanced simple delta design, and Lockheed coming up also with a delta shape, but the engines grouped both above and below the wing.

In Europe, Aérospatiale began a study in 1974 for a possible 'Concorde B', which would draw on the lessons learnt first time around and make use of newer technology, especially in the field of lighter materials. But the slump in the airline market led to the abandonment of the project in June 1976. A month before, BAC had proposed an initial two-year study to establish the engineering and environmental parameters of an advanced supersonic transport (AST), and this was taken a step further together with Aerospatiale and McDonnell Douglas as an American partner. In December 1978, the three companies

(BAC meanwhile had become part of British Aerospace) published their views on the prospects for such an aircraft, which they said was feasible and could be in service by 1990. NASA was approached in February 1980 to participate in joint technological experiments, to which it eventually agreed to, but a severe cut in its aeronautics budget by the new Reagan administration forced the cancellation of the joint project, as well as its own SCR programme.

But that was not the end of it. With the popularity of Concorde after entering service in 1976, and the failure of its own machinations to stop the aircraft landing on its soil, it was inevitable that the United States would soon want to wrest back the lead it had handed to the Europeans in SST technology. Where it had missed out the first time, it wanted to make doubly sure that it was in the vanguard of future generation SST development. President Reagan's budget priorities soon gave way to more expansive ideas for US supremacy in the air and in space. In 1983, the US Government's Office of Science and Technology Policy (OSTP) commissioned an aeronautical policy review committee, which comprised 16 leading figures

BELOW: McDonnell Douglas HSCT concept of the 1980s.

TOP RIGHT: Boeing HSCT concept.

BELOW RIGHT: Aérospatiale Alliance second-generation SST evolved from its collaboration with an international working group.

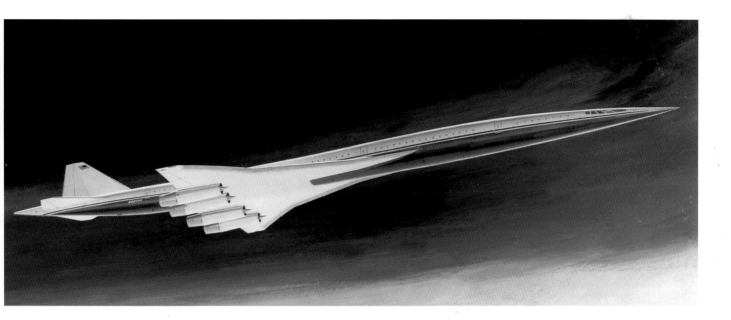

from government, industry and academia. By 1985, the OSTP had formulated a policy, which proposed three national goals for aeronautical research and development, one of which was the development of technologies for a future long-range supersonic transport.

In response to OSTP recommendations, NASA initiated contractual and internal studies for a High Speed Civil Transport (HSCT). It issued contracts to both Boeing and McDonnell Douglas in 1986, tasking the two companies to address two major issues:

• Is it technically possible to build an environmentally-acceptable second-generation SST, and could it be economically competitive with the new-generation long-range subsonic transports then on the drawing board.

In particular, three environmental goals had to be satisfied for an HSCT to be acceptable:
• The HSCT must have no significant effect on the ozone layer;
• HSCT community noise must meet the equivalent of current FAR 36 Stage 3 requirements;
• There can be no perceptible boom over populated areas.

In 1989, NASA launched the $284 million industry-government High Speed Research Program (HSRP) to develop the technologies required to realise these goals. For a time, Mach 5 hypersonics intruded into SST discussions after Reagan talked up the National Aero-Space Plane (NASP) by suggesting that it could also be developed into a hypersonic 'Orient Express' airliner. British Aerospace also toyed for a while with its HOTOL (horizontal take-off and landing) concept, which, although intended to carry satellites into orbit, was also suggested as a

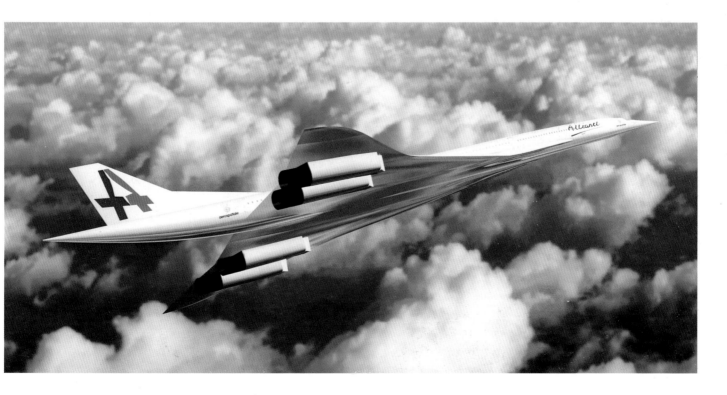

hypersonic transport which could reduce flying time between Britain and Australia to under one hour.

With significant technological advances made in the 1970s and 1980s in the areas of light-weight, high-strength materials, computational fluid dynamics, flight control systems, variable-cycle propulsion and high-speed computers, coupled with projected high traffic growth in the trans-Atlantic and Pacific Rim markets, both Boeing and McDonnell Douglas made encouraging noises. In its market studies, Boeing concluded that appropriate HSCT routes would be those between North America and the Far East, North America and Europe, and between Europe and the Far East. Eliminating predominantly overland routes, because of the yet to be solved sonic boom problems, and routes shorter than 2,500 nautical miles (4,625km), it put the potential market for an HSCT at between 1,000 and 1,500 units, 'sufficient to justify further study.'

McDonnell Douglas suggested that as much as 20 percent of traffic demand by 2010 could be met with HSCT-type aircraft. But it also recognised that any fleet size projections were highly sensitive to 'elasticity of fares.' Its study indicated that an estimated 1,500-strong HSCT fleet may be commercially viable by 2030 with a 20 percent fare premium, which it stated 'represents significant marketing and production potential for Douglas in particular and the aerospace industry in general.' Based on a potential supersonic network over 250 international city pairs, Douglas concluded that the design mission require-ment would be 5,500nm (10,175km), with 25 percent being flown at subsonic speeds (Mach 0.95) because of environmental considerations. This range capability, it added, would be adequate for more than 90 percent of the selected city pairs.

Boeing selected a design range of 5,000nm (9,250km) for the initial baseline aircraft, which, according to its own evaluation, covered more than 50 percent of the 234 city pairs studied, if flown non-stop. A design range of 6,500nm, it added, would capture approximately 85 percent of the non-stop revenue passenger-miles in the HSCT market, but this would make the aircraft heavy and expensive. However, downstream improve-ments in propulsion and structure technologies would, said Boeing, allow the HSCT to 'grow' into longer non-stop range markets. Both companies accepted that, while the economic and operational outlook for the aircraft would be enhanced if restrictions on supersonic overland flights would be lifted, it would require considerable improvements in technologies and changes in government regulations for that to become reality. Consequently, both considered aircraft configured to fly subsonically overland, while continuing parallel design studies into concepts that would enable aircraft to fly supersonically over populated areas.

BOEING VERSUS DOUGLAS

The design engineers at Douglas settled on an aircraft capable of carrying 300 passengers over a distance of 5,500 nautical miles, at a speed of Mach 2.4. The gross weight was in the 700,000–800,000lb (317,500–362,900kg) range. An alternative concept, cruising at a lower Mach 1.6, which places fewer demands on the thermal and material productivity, was also being studied, although the Mach 2.4 aircraft was given priority. McDonnell Douglas contended that a slower aircraft cruising at a lower altitude of 45,000ft (13,700m) would halve the ozone depletion for the projected fleet sizes.

By and large, the structure, materials and other design features were similar for both concepts, but the projected Mach 1.6 aircraft had a much smaller wing of a straight delta shape, compared to the double-delta planform of the Mach 2.4 HSCT. The time scale for the HSCT envisaged a first flight in 2003, certification in 2005, and an in service date of 2006. The likely purchase price of the HSCT was assessed at around two to three times that of an equivalent subsonic aircraft.

The airframe structural design was based on materials with potential or known long-term thermal stability and adequate mechanical properties at sustained high temperatures, minimum material density, and the ability to be fabricated and assembled at minimum cost. These were identified to be titanium, discrete-reinforced, elevated-temperature aluminium, and high-temperature polymeric composites (HPC). Douglas stated, however, that years of work remained before a final material could be selected with confidence.

For the baseline aircraft, therefore, an optimisation process, which deter-mined structural forces by a 125-point MINIVER aerothermal and a NASTRAN finite-element analysis, produced a design that featured a combination of different materials.

LEFT: British Aerospace AST.

TOP RIGHT: Types of engine evaluated by Boeing as part of its HSCT studies.

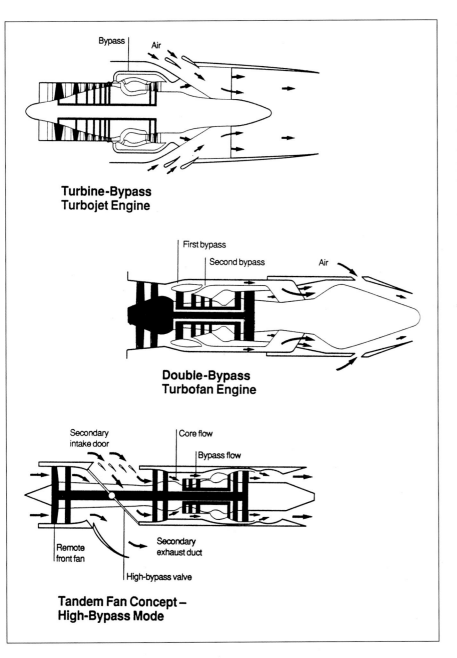

**Turbine-Bypass
Turbojet Engine**

**Double-Bypass
Turbofan Engine**

**Tandem Fan Concept –
High-Bypass Mode**

the wing substructure webs, spars and trusses were to be constructed from HPC. In order to minimise forces created from the inevitable thermal mismatches (because of the fuel in the wings and shielding of parts of the fuselage by the wing), Douglas incorporated a number of longitudinal expansion joints in the inboard portion of the wing. These joints provided a de-coupling of the wing from fuselage bending loads and axial thermal growth, while maintaining an effective shear tie and aerodynamically smooth connection across each section.

The wing leading edges were initially designed as a full-depth titanium honeycomb sandwich, with the control surfaces and flaps as thin-skin, postbuckled multirib HPC boxes. However, further optimisation studies were to be conducted before a final decision.

Unlike the wing, the fuselage was optimised to a single mode of construction and material to achieve minimum weight and cost, consisting of a Z-stiffened HPC shell, where the frame is clipped to the skin with glass-reinforced polymer composite shear ties. An alternative construction evaluated for weight reduction was an HPC pseudo-monocoque isogrid shell in the pressurised fuselage, although such construction was considered economical only in a constant-section fuselage, whereas the design favoured a body based on the area rule premise.

Four engine cycles and variants were assessed, based on their installed noise and performance. The Pratt & Whitney variable-stream control engine (VSCE) was evaluated with convergent divergent ejector and high-flow mixer ejector nozzles, but was eliminated early on because of high noise and low performance. The General Electric variable-cycle engine (VCE) was selected for further consideration because of good performance, although additional noise reduction schemes needed to be incorporated. In the final analysis, however, the GE three-stream exhaust non-augmented high-flow fan (FLA) and the P&W non-augmented turbine bypass engine (TBE) with a convergent divergent ejector nozzle and chute suppressor, were considered to be the quietest of the four and to have the best overall performance. The two engine manufacturers subsequently decided to pool resources, and the two concepts, plus a mixed-flow turbofan (MFTF) were chosen for further study, with performance data expected to be available in late 1991 or early 1992.

The baseline wing was split into four distinct regions. The low-sweep, high aspect-ratio outboard panel utilised a conventional multi-spar, multi-rib structural box, optimised with high-temperature polymer composite (HPC) honeycomb sandwich cover panels. A transition bulkhead attached the outboard panel to the aft wing box, which was an unswept beam running across the aircraft supporting the outboard wing panel, engines, main landing gear, and the rear end of the mid wing. Being primarily strength-critical, the aft wing box was covered with four-sheet titanium panels. The mid-wing region was cut away to provide space for gear stowage, serving primarily as a bridge between the outboard portions of the aft wing box and the forward strake. It was optimised as a cellular raft with HPC honeycomb sandwich cover panels.

The fourth part of the wing was the large and highly swept, but lightly stressed strake, which comprised a transverse carry-through box, supporting the forward section of the mid wing and redistributed the landing gear loads. Most of the strake was cantilevered from the side of the fuselage. A high proportion of

With the aircraft wing area and thrust established at take-off condition, Douglas recommended a high-lift system comprising leading and trailing edge flaps, and computer-controlled high-lift setting changes during take-off and initial climb to maximise performance. It was also anticipated that the same system would be used at different settings during the sub-sonic climb and cruise sectors. Analytical and experimental studies were aimed at achieving a lift-to-drag ratio of 8 at second-segment climb conditions. The flight control concept was based on fly-by-light/power-by-wire, eliminating a central hydraulic system, with all functions performed by electric and/or electro-hydraulic servo pump actuators. The flightdeck was designed around a panoramic wide-screen panel display synthesised from remote sensors, thus eliminating the mechanical deflection of the nose to increase pilot visibility during the low-speed, high-angle-of attack operation, as used on Concorde. Such a display has the added advantage of enhancing operations in poor visibility or at night.

Boeing studies conducted under the NASA contract evaluated 21 configurations designed for Mach numbers between 2.4 and 10.0, but these were whittled down to six after a screening process that assessed risk versus benefits. These six were further developed and analysed, with the conclusion that speeds above Mach 3.2 would be impractical, as aircraft size and complexity increase significantly. As a result, subsequent studies narrowed the speed range down to between Mach 2.4 and 3.2, and still further to an envelope bounded by Mach 2.0 and 2.5, which was considered the optimum for a commercial HSCT. This speed region was additionally supported by the relationship between the average Mach number and cruise Mach number. So, after four years of design evolution, Boeing

TOP: Digital simulation by French research agency Onera of Alliance model, indicating airflow over wing leading edge and wing tips.

BELOW: The Japanese industry favoured a Mach 2.5 design capable of carrying 400 passengers non-stop between Tokyo and New York.

designers proceeded on the basis of a Mach 2.4 HSCT, with a maximum take-off weight of 700,000lb (317,500kg) and capable of carrying 300 passengers a distance of 5,000 nautical miles, much the same as their counterparts at Douglas.

Structurally, Boeing also proceeded along similar lines to Douglas, but examined other performance-enhancing concepts such as increasing vortex lift to improve low-speed performance, and laminar flow control (LFC) for reduced aero-dynamic drag. Research into both was conducted jointly with NASA, with the US Air Force also involved in the laminar flow flight tests conducted on a Boeing 757. In Europe, Airbus Industrie conducted LFC flight tests on an A320. Laminar flow is aimed at reducing aerodynamic drag through tiny skin perforations in the wing leading edges, tail unit and engine nacelles. These micro-holes maintain the airflow in the vicinity of the aircraft in the laminar state and delay its transition to the

ABOVE: Lockheed promoted a liquid-hydrogen fuelled four-engined SST, which would cruise at Mach 2.7 and carry 234 passengers a distance of 4,200 nautical miles.

LEFT: Windtunnel testing of European second-generation SST.

BELOW: As part of NASA's supersonic cruise research program (SCR) in the mid-1970s, Lockheed came up with an interesting design, attaching the engines above and below the wing.

turbulent stage, effectively reducing skin friction drag, which accounts for around 40 percent of the total aerodynamic drag on high-speed aircraft. Developing low sonic boom technology was also high on the agenda in its work with NASA, using both emerging analysis and wind tunnel testing methods, although so far, no satisfactory design to limit supersonic noise to an acceptable level has been possible. A re-shaping of the fuselage and wing, and advanced ejector-suppressor engine nozzles and inlet designs, have yet to be validated.

INTERNATIONAL COLLABORATION

In parallel with their own studies, both Boeing and McDonnell Douglas also joined an international study group, the Supersonic Commercial Transport (SCT) group, formed in May 1990 to explore criteria and issues involved in developing a second-generation SST. The initial study group, which also included Aérospatiale, British Aerospace and Deutsche Airbus, was the result of recognition by the industry that, because of the financial requirements and risks, a new SST would most probably have to be a joint endeavour. In the following year, the group was enlarged with the addition of the Society of Japanese Aerospace Companies (SJAC), Alenia of Italy and Russia's Tupolev OKB.

The target for the group was to launch the pre-development programme by 1999, with a first flight in 2005, and entry into service before 2010. That was the date Concorde was to be withdrawn from service, although life extension programmes have pushed that date out to 2017. Interestingly, perceived market requirements have taken most manufacturers down similar roads when defining a baseline aircraft for further development.

Designs for a successor to Concorde had been on the drawing boards at Aérospatiale (now part of EADS) for a long time. Known as the ATSF (Avion de Transport Supersonique Futur), it crystallised into a 200-seat Mach 2+ aircraft, with an initial range of 5,500 nautical miles (10,00km+) to provide trans-Pacific capability, going up to 6,500nm (12,000km) later on. One of the main aims was to bring operating costs down to a level which would enable airlines to offer fares comparable to existing first class, and possibly even business-class. It was intended to be in service around the turn of the century. Upon joining the SCT, the project was refined in collaboration with the French aerospace research agency Onera and engine maker SNECMA into the Alliance, a 250–300-seat, 661,387lb (300,000kg) aircraft with a range of 8,835 miles (11,000km), and featuring a high-aspect ratio double-delta wing and area ruling to reduce supersonic drag. The British Aerospace Advanced Supersonic Transport (AST) was similar in size, but differed in employing a lower wing aspect ratio and a canard foreplane to improve pitch control and reduce trim drag.

In April 1994, Aérospatiale, British Aerospace and Deutsche Aerospace (Dasa) signed a Memorandum of Understanding (MoU) for a jointly-funded European project, effectively melding the individual conceptual studies into a single project, within the framework of the European Supersonic Research Program (ESRP). The design goals included a take-off weight not exceeding 716,502lb (325,000kg), the ability to

cruise at Mach 2+ for up to six hours, and space for 250–300 passengers, not that dissimilar from the US designs. The joint project featured a constant cross-section circular fuselage, rather than an area rule 'waisted' cross-section, with Canard foreplanes and a double-delta wing.

As to the proposed power plant, the European research, unlike that in the United States, is based on a dual-core, variable-cycle fanjet, dubbed the MTF (Mid-Tandem Fan), essentially a merging of the SNECMA MCV99 concept and the Rolls-Royce Tandem Fan, which the two companies had been working on since 1989. MTU and Fiat Avio were subsequently brought in to the team. The louvre-type auxiliary air inlets supply air to a secondary fan between the LP and HP compressors, hence the term 'mid-tandem'. This increases the total airflow to the engine, which in turn decreases gas exhaust velocity, and, therefore, noise. Delivering about 50,000lb (222.5kN) thrust, the variable-cycle MTF is said to satisfy the stringent fuel consumption criteria at all speeds, as well as strict international noise and pollution standards. Ultimately, the design team aims for a 50 percent reduction in fuel consumption, an 80 percent reduction in nitrous oxides — already achieved in engine combustion work — and noise levels of 18dB below the current Stage 3 limits.

Apart from Aérospatiale and British Aerospace, the only other manufacturer with operational experience of supersonic aircraft, Tupolev, also felt that the time was right for a second-generation SST and began studying possible configurations in 1988 in collaboration with the TsAGI and GosNII research institutions. Tupolev's design, designated Tu-244, had a more highly swept and larger double-delta wing, but mirrored in overall size, capacity and performance, the baseline aircraft proposed by the other manufacturers. Although no details were given on the powerplant, the aircraft was expected to be powered by four 72,800lb (324kN) turbofans, possibly derived from the Kuznetsov NK-231. Two versions were planned, one for trans-Atlantic services with a range of 4,660 miles (7,500km) and seating for 450 passengers, the other for Pacific flights with a range of 5,748 miles (9,250km) and a passenger capacity of 300.

Tupolev continues to use the Tu-144LL as a flying laboratory to test and validate its research in support of the Tu-244, with some flight test programmes undertaken in conjunction with NASA. Tupolev had planned to put the aircraft into service in 2010, envisaging a world market for 500–1200 units, but no further details have been released. In parallel, it was also working on the Tu-2000, a Mach 6 hypersonic spaceplane, but it has also gone quiet on that front.

With funding provided by the Ministry of International Trade and Industry (MITI), Japan set up a SST/HST (hypersonic transport) study committee in 1987, with the aim of having a supersonic aircraft in the air by 2005 and a hypersonic (Mach 5) aircraft in the 2020–2030 timeframe. The Committee, set up within the Society of Japanese Aerospace Companies (SJAC), was comprised of aircraft manufacturers (Fuji, Kawasaki, Mitsubishi), engine manufacturer Ishikawajima Harima (IHI), airlines (Japan Airlines and All Nippon Airways), the National Aerospace Laboratory (NAL), the

Evolution des configurations étudiées à Aerospatiale entre 1979-1989
History of configuration studies at Aerospatiale (1979-1989)

CONCORDE	ATSF 1	ATSF 2	ATSF 3

1ER VOL
FIRST FLIGHT

1969	1978	1983	1989

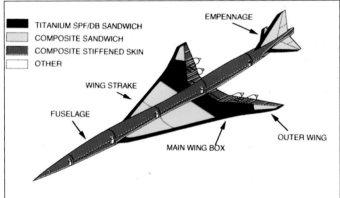

■ TITANIUM SPF/DB SANDWICH
▨ COMPOSITE SANDWICH
■ COMPOSITE STIFFENED SKIN
□ OTHER

EMPENNAGE

WING STRAKE

FUSELAGE

OUTER WING

MAIN WING BOX

TOP: Aérospatiale configuration studies 1979-1989.

ABOVE: McDonnell Douglas baseline aircraft showing materials used in its construction.

LEFT: Windtunnel tests of Boeing HSCT model.

Engineering Research Association for Super/Hypersonic Transport Propulsion Systems (HYPR) and the Research & Development Institute of Metals and Composites for Future Industries (RIMCOF).

The baseline study focused on a 300-seat SST with a take-off weight of 992,080lb (450,000kg) and a speed of around Mach 2.5. An upper range limit of 6,500nm (12,000km) was set. The wing and fuselage were first designed in metal, but composites were later substituted to provide a one quarter saving in weight. Both a single fan engine with sound suppresser and a tandem fan without suppresser were considered, aiming at a community noise level of 5dB below FAR Stage 3 requirements. The notional Mach 5 HST was also designed with 300 seats, a 6,500nm range, and a cruising altitude of 90,000ft (27,500m). One of the principal efforts towards that goal was a hypersonic propulsion research programme, which also included Pratt & Whitney, General Electric, Rolls-Royce and SNECMA.

This programme focused on a combined-cycle turbofan/ramjet engine, where the turbofan produces all the thrust up to around Mach 2.5, and the ramjet above Mach 3.0, with the transition between the two taking place between Mach 2.5 and 3.0. Turbofan thrust was envisaged at 60,000lb (267kN) at sea level, with the ramjet producing 26,000lb (115kN) at Mach 5 cruise. A sub-scale test engine with about 6,600lb (30kN) sea level thrust, designated HYPR 90-T, began ground tests at IHI's Mizuho plant in December 1994, and these were followed in 1996 by altitude tests conducted by General Electric, and by open-air noise tests by Rolls-Royce in 1997.

SETBACK

The quest for a successor to Concorde received a considerable setback when Boeing, which had taken over McDonnell Douglas, decided in late 1998 to put its HSCT studies on the backburner. The official reasons given were technical issues involved in meeting proposed future Stage 4 noise levels, and a shift in market projections. Taking its lead from its key industry partner, NASA abandoned its HSR programme in January 1999, together with four further test flights with the Tupolev Tu-144, which were due to begin at Zhukovsky on 24 February.

As a result, the target in-service date was pushed back another ten years, to at least 2020. However, with $35 million government funding, the US Defense Advanced Research Projects Agency (DARPA) has launched the Quiet Supersonic Platform (QSP) programme, which could have applications in the commercial market. The two-year programme goals include a supersonic lift-to-drag ratio of 11, engine thrust-to-weight ratio of 7.5, specific fuel consumption of 1.05lb/lb/h, and compliance with Stage 3 noise limits. But the single most important objective is the reduction of the sonic boom to a ground signature initial shock strength of no more than $0.3\text{lb}/\text{ft}^2$ ($1.9\text{mbar}/\text{m}^2$), which is assumed would be the level acceptable to the public for supersonic travel across land.

Independently, Nevada-based Reno Aeronautical is working on a Mach 1.5 business jet powered by two Pratt & Whitney JT8D-219 turbofans, with a gross weight of 110,000lb (50,000kg) and a range of almost 6,000nm (11,000km).

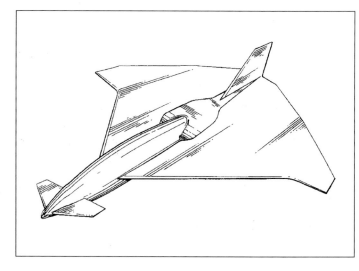

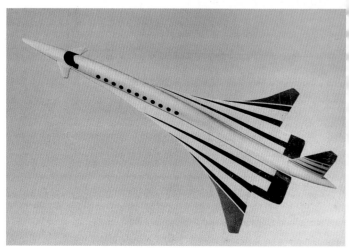

TOP: In the Tu-244 Tupolev opted for a 300-passenger aircraft with a cruise speed of Mach 2.05.

ABOVE CENTRE: Sukhoi S-51 SSBJ.

ABOVE: A possible SSBJ configuration advanced by Lockheed shows a double-canard and gull wing design, with a central variable-cycle engine installation.

TOP RIGHT: Diagrammatic representation of the variable-cycle fanjet dubbed the MTF (mid-tandem fan) considered for the European SST.

OPPOSITE PAGE, BELOW LEFT: Gulfstream/Sukhoi SSBJ.

OPPOSITE PAGE, BELOW RIGHT: Three-view drawing of the Tu-244.

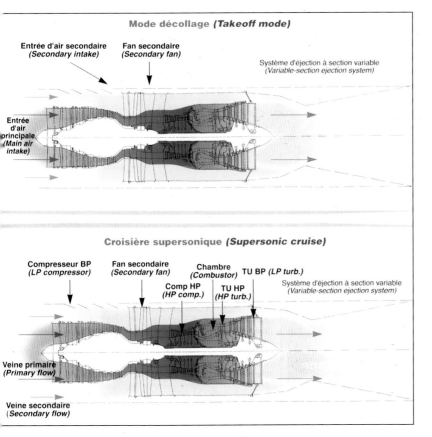

Mode décollage (Takeoff mode)

Entrée d'air secondaire (Secondary intake)
Fan secondaire (Secondary fan)
Système d'éjection à section variable (Variable-section ejection system)
Entrée d'air principale (Main air intake)

Croisière supersonique (Supersonic cruise)

Compresseur BP (LP compressor)
Fan secondaire (Secondary fan)
Comp HP (HP comp.)
Chambre (Combustor)
TU HP (HP turb.)
TU BP (LP turb.)
Système d'éjection à section variable (Variable-section ejection system)
Veine primaire (Primary flow)
Veine secondaire (Secondary flow)

mounted turbofan engines of 12,000lb (53.4kN) thrust each, probably derived from military power plants, a cranked delta wing and canard foreplanes, and an ovoid cabin for eight passengers. Other features included a synthetic system for maximum crew vision at high angles of attack, and automatic fuel trimming. Length was 104ft (31.70m), wingspan 55ft 7½in (16.95m), and a maximum take-off weight 86,000lb (39,000kg). Speed was given as Mach 1.8, and range at 4,000nm (7,400km). Dassault, however, acknowledged at that time that the question of a suitable power plant compliant with Stage 3 noise requirements remained unsolved, forcing it to abandon its studies in March 1999.

On a more positive note, EADS Airbus (formerly Aérospatiale Matra) believes that a new supersonic transport aircraft could be flying by 2015, although the speed is likely to be less than that of Concorde. However, 2020 would appear to be the most likely earliest date. But, before even that becomes reality, operating costs will have to come down dramatically, and the sonic boom problem needs to be resolved. Unless that can be achieved, the SSBJ could well beat the second-generation SST into the air.

Technical feasibility and market studies are being conducted. Gulfstream had previously been involved with Russia's Sukhoi Design Bureau in the three-engined S-21 SSBJ, which projected a Mach 2.0 speed and a supersonic range of 4,000nm (7,400km), very similar to the present studies with Lockheed. Engine definition was being undertaken by Rolls-Royce in conjunction with the Soviet Lyulka Design Bureau. This joint project of 1989 died a quick death, and it was Dassault Aviation, which re-ignited interest in SSBJs, when it announced at the September 1997 NBAA conference that it was looking into the feasibility of a SSBJ. It had discussions with Boeing, but found little interest from the Seattle-based manufacturer and decided to go it alone. Based on its successful Falcon range, preliminary designs for the Falcon SST showed three rear-

At a lecture in London in 1993, Bob McKinlay, then chairman of British Aerospace Airbus, said he believed strongly that there will be a supersonic successor to Concorde. But he also added that 'grandfathers are not going to want to say to their grandchildren: we used to cross the Atlantic in three and a half hours.' Present indications are that they may well have to say just that. A hypersonic aircraft, which potentially could connect London with Sydney in three hours, is still some 50 years away.

Beyond that lies the realm of the spaceplane, which is basically a manned, re-usable single-stage-to-orbit (SSTO) transportation system with speeds in excess of Mach 7, and capable of take-off and landing from conventional runways. But to Concorde must go the credit for starting it all.

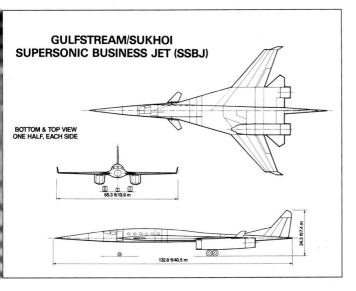

GULFSTREAM/SUKHOI SUPERSONIC BUSINESS JET (SSBJ)

BOTTOM & TOP VIEW ONE HALF, EACH SIDE

65.3 ft/19.9 m

132.8 ft/40.5 m

24.3 ft/7.4 m

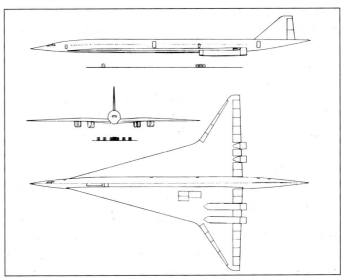

TOP: In the 1980s, Aérospatiale worked on a Mach 2-2.5 design referred to as the Avion de Transport Supersonique du Futur (ATSF). It later became known as the Alliance, but changed very little.

LEFT: NASA engine intake noise-reduction tests. *NASA*

BELOW LEFT: Japan's Kawasaki has exhibited its latest design in model form.

ABOVE CENTRE: Lack of a suitable propulsion system has forced Dassault to halt its plans for a SSBJ based on its successful Falcon range.

ABOVE: National Aerospace Laboratory (NAL) in Japan is promoting this design for an SST.

TOP RIGHT: Windtunnel tests of Boeing HSCT model.

OPPOSITE PAGE, BELOW LEFT: External vision system (EVS) examined as part of NASA's high-speed research. *NASA/Langley Research Centre*

OPPOSITE PAGE, BELOW RIGHT: The shape of the next-generation SST? *NASA/Langley Research Center*

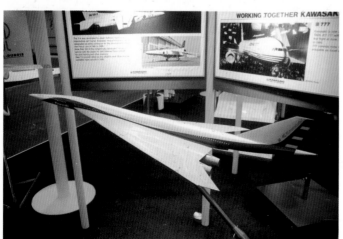

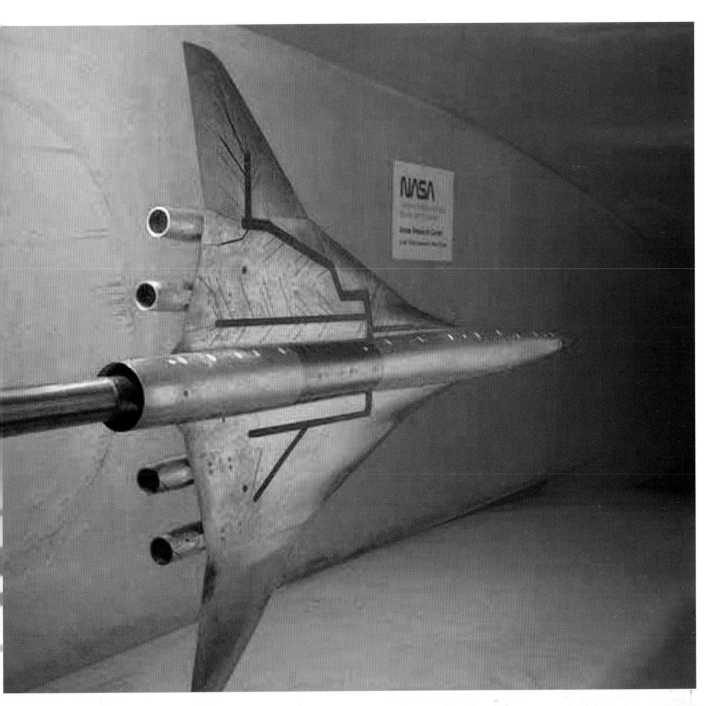

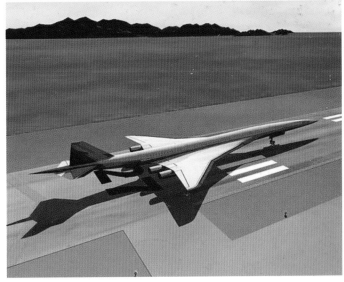

9 ACCIDENTS AND INCIDENTS

In nearly 25 years of sustained service, no supersonic transport had been lost with fare-paying passengers on board — a record unmatched by any other commercial aircraft — until an Air France Concorde went down in flames two minutes after take-off from Paris in a crash that shocked the world.

Concorde had suffered some minor mishaps over the period, as had the Tu-144 in its much shorter service history, but the tragic loss of 113 people on 25 July 2000 provoked extraordinary reactions across the world. Major news channels interrupted their programmes and broadcast updates on reports coming out of the crash site for days after, and at Farnborough, where the world's aerospace industry met for the biennial air show, flags were flown at half mast.

No accident of any other type of aircraft would have generated so much publicity or emotion, but then, Concorde is an exceptional aircraft, and the world's only supersonic passenger transport. As such, it has achieved icon status, and its fallibility was inevitably viewed as a tragedy, in more than one sense. Headline writers tried to out do each other, but predictions of the end of Concorde and supersonic operations were somewhat premature, in spite of the hopefully temporary withdrawal of the aircraft's operating certificate.

In the wake of the crash, all previous incidents involving Concorde were aired in the media, which gave rise to much speculation and suggested tenuous links to the cause of the accident. Among these were the appearance of hairline cracks in the wing spar of a British Airways aircraft, discovered two days before the day of the crash and led to the grounding of that particular aircraft, and three emergency landings due to engine troubles earlier in 2000. Together with reports of poor tyre wear and several tyre bursts throughout its service life, these incidents fuelled the imagination of reporters, resulting in untold damage to Concorde's reputation.

Other incidents highlighted were the return to Heathrow of a New York-bound flight on 26 May 1998 after a large elevon became dislodged from the wing, and the shattering of three outer windows during a check flight, which could have led to a

BELOW: Concorde flight AF4590 flight profile. *Gareth Burgess/Flight International*

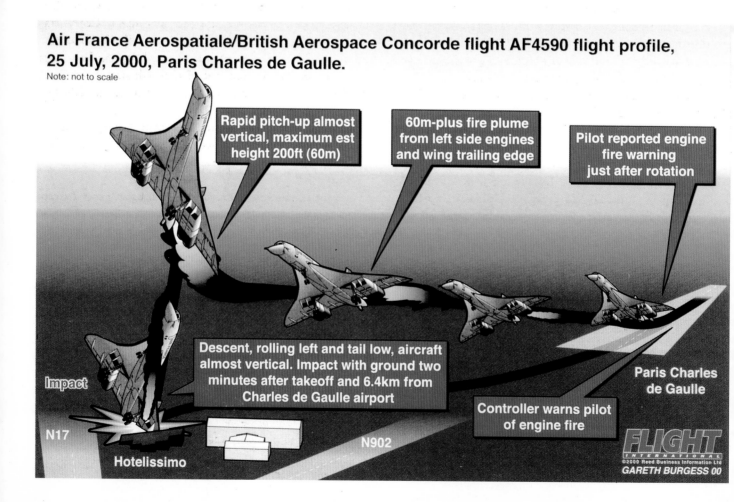

Air France Aerospatiale/British Aerospace Concorde flight AF4590 flight profile, 25 July, 2000, Paris Charles de Gaulle.
Note: not to scale

Rapid pitch-up almost vertical, maximum est height 200ft (60m)

60m-plus fire plume from left side engines and wing trailing edge

Pilot reported engine fire warning just after rotation

Descent, rolling left and tail low, aircraft almost vertical. Impact with ground two minutes after takeoff and 6.4km from Charles de Gaulle airport

Controller warns pilot of engine fire

Paris Charles de Gaulle

Impact

N17

Hotelissimo

N902

FLIGHT INTERNATIONAL
©2000 Reed Business Information Ltd
GARETH BURGESS 00

potentially catastrophic cabin depressurisation. Less was made of an already much publicised event in 1992, when a large section of rudder fell into the Atlantic.

FIERY ROUTE TO DISASTER

The sight of a Concorde blazing uncontrollably, shot by an amateur photographer and filling TV screens around the world, contributed greatly to the sense of personal loss felt by many people. When the Air France Concorde F-BTSC lined up on the runway at Paris Charles de Gaulle Airport on 25 July 2000, the 100, mostly German, passengers were looking forward to start their Latin American cruise holiday aboard the luxury liner MS *Deutschland* with a chartered supersonic flight to New York. Flight AF4590 was somewhat late in leaving, initially due to the delayed arrival of baggage from Germany, and then by the replacement of the No.2 engine's faulty thrust reverser, demanded by the aircraft's captain Christian Marty, a highly experience pilot with 32 years flying experience. Much was made of this in the subsequent clamour for explanations of the crash, but the engine makers Rolls-Royce and SNECMA insisted that the aircraft can fly safely without a functioning reverser.

At 4:42 pm local time, Flight 4590 was cleared by the control tower for take-off. Captain Marty was at the controls, assisted by co-pilot Jean Marcot. As Concorde hurtled down the runway flames were shooting apparently from a left engine, which spread quickly to engulf the whole of the left wing, trailing thick black smoke. Captain Marty reported an engine fire warning in the cockpit, and some 56 seconds after clearance for take-off, he was alerted by the tower to the danger. But by then the aircraft had reached V1 and was travelling too fast to abort the take-off. Captain Marty confirmed failure of the No.2 engine, but added that he would proceed to get airborne and attempt an emergency landing at nearby Le Bourget.

The aircraft did get airborne, but failed to gain any significant height. The Concorde's flight data recorder later revealed that the second of the left bank of engines failed, with No.1 engine operating intermittently, and Marty also reported that he was unable to retract the landing gear, greatly affecting the aerodynamic stability of the aircraft. Desperate attempts to pull up the nose to gain altitude resulted in a stall, causing the aircraft to roll to the left and, in an almost vertical attitude, back slide down towards the ground.

Just two minutes after take-off, the Concorde impacted the small Hotelissimo hotel at Gonesse, some 3.7 miles (6km) from the end of the runway, killing all 100 passengers and the crew of nine, as well as four hotel employees on the ground. The aircraft and an annexe of the hotel were virtually obliterated by the explosion. The myth of the invincibility of the big white bird had been shattered and all Air France Concordes were grounded immediately. F-BTSC, the third production aircraft, first flew on 31 January 1975. At the time of the crash it had logged 11,989 flight hours and 3,978 flight cycles.

The size of the fire and smoke plume, which extended some 200ft (60m) from the engine and wing trailing edge, initially suggested that a catastrophic engine failure had taken place, possibly in combination with ruptured fuel lines. Other, more fanciful theories put forward in the immediate aftermath included a possible terrorist bomb, and problems with the afterburners on the Olympus turbojet engines. Some of the media also engaged in deplorable mischief-making by examining the fast and sporty lifestyle of the Concorde's captain.

Within hours, however, the investigation shifted towards a possible tyre burst late in the take-off run, which could have resulted in tyre debris puncturing fuel lines in the wheel well and finding its way into the engine intake. Experts also speculated that a metal strip on the runway caused a tyre to explode. This metal strip, identified as a thrust reverser cover, was later found to have come from a Continental Airlines DC-10, which had taken off from Charles de Gaulle a few minutes before Concorde. Not surprisingly, the thrust reverser repair and the Air France mechanics also came under close scrutiny — a criminal investigation for manslaughter was even officially launched — although any causal link was quickly discounted.

Another issue uppermost in the mind of the French accident investigation bureau, the Bureau Equêtes d'Accidents (BEA), was that of the water deflector, which it said was among the debris found on the runway. Made of toughened fibreglass, the deflectors were designed to prevent surface water being ingested by the adjacent engine intakes. A broken water deflector had been specifically implicated in a British tyre burst incident in October 1993, which prompted the UK Air Accident Investigation Branch (AAIB) to state that debris from a broken deflector was 'almost certainly' responsible for the airframe damage.

As the certainty grew that a tyre burst had been the primary cause, Concorde's certificate of airworthiness (CofA) was suspended on 16 August. In a letter to the UK Civil Aviation Authority (CAA) from Ken Smart, the AAIB's Chief Inspector of Air Accidents, the recommendation to suspend the CofA was based on the following facts, which had been established by that date:

- During the take-off run the front tyre of the left main landing gear was destroyed between V1 and VR, very probably because it ran over a piece of metal.

- The destruction of the tyre has caused damage, either directly or indirectly, to the aircraft structure and systems, leading to the crash less than one minute and 30 seconds after the destruction of the tyre.

The damage sequence and the links between various events had not then been fully established, but the letter went on to list a number of subsequent events, including:

- One, or more punctures of at least one fuel tank with a major fuel leak.

- Ignition of the leaking fuel and an intense fire which lasted for the duration of the flight, the fire appeared within a few seconds of the destruction of the tyre.

- The loss of thrust in one, and then two engines.

When the preliminary report was released by the French BEA on 31 August 2000, a tyre burst was indeed given as the cause of setting in train a chain of events, which brought down the aircraft. The judicial enquiry into why it happened was not due to be completed until late in 2001. The report stated that 'the July 25 accident shows that the destruction of a tyre, an event that we cannot say will not recur, had catastrophic consequences in a short period of time, preventing the crew from rectifying the situation.'

The BEA also confirmed that a 17in (430mm) x 1in (25mm) riveted metal strip had been found on the runway. This was later identified to have come from a Continental Airlines DC-10-30 and given as the most likely reason for the tyre burst.

The transcript of the conversation between the tower and the flight crew onboard Concorde illustrates with chilling clarity that for the crew, while at first unaware that anything was amiss and then trying everything under impossible circumstances, time had run out.

Controller: Air France 4590, runway 26 right, wind zero 90 knots, takeoff authorised (*4:42 pm local time*)

Co-pilot: 4590 taking off 26 right (*sound of switch*).

Pilot: Is everyone ready?

Co-pilot: Yes.

Engineer: Yes.

Pilot: Up to 100, 150 (*followed by unclear words, sound of switch*). Top (*noise similar to engines increasing power*).

Unidentified voice: (*on radio Channel*) Go on, Christian.

Engineer: We have four heated up (*sound of switch*).

Co-pilot: 100 knots.

Pilot: Confirmed.

Engineer: Four green.

Co-pilot: V one (*low-frequency noise*).

Pilot: (*unclear*)

Co-pilot: Watch out.

Controller: Concorde zero . . . 4590, you have flames (*unclear*) you have flames behind you.

Unidentified voice: (*simultaneously on radio*) Right. (*background noise changes, sound of switch*).

Engineer: Stop (*unclear*).

Co-pilot: Well received.

Engineer: Breakdown, eng . . . breakdown engine two (*two sounds of switches, followed by fire alarm*).

Unidentified voice: (*on radio*) It's burning badly, huh (*Gong*).

Engineer: Cut engine two.

Pilot: Engine fire procedure (*sound of switch, end of ringing*).

Co-pilot: Warning, the airspeed indicator, the airspeed indicator, the airspeed indicator (*sound of switch, gong*).

Person in tower: It's burning badly and I'm not sure it's coming from the engine (*switch sound similar to fire extinguisher handle being activated*).

Pilot: Gear on the way up.

Controller: 4590, you have strong flames behind you.

Engineer: The gear (*alarm, similar to toilet smoke alert*).

Controller: Beginning reception of a Middle Marker.

Co-pilot: Yes, well received.

Engineer: The gear, no (*Gong*).

Controller: So, at your convenience, you have priority to land.

Engineer: Gear.

Co-pilot: No (*two switch noises*).

Pilot: Gear (*unclear*), coming up.

Co-pilot: Well received (*fire alarm, gong, three switch sounds*).

Co-pilot: I'm trying (*unclear*).

Engineer: I'm hitting.

Pilot: Are (*unclear*) you cutting engine two (*end of smoke alarm*).

Engineer: I've cut it.

Controller: End reception Middle Marker.

Co-pilot: The airspeed indicator (*sound of switch, end of ringing*).

Co-pilot: The gear won't come up (*fire alarm rings*).

Aircraft instrument: WHOOP WHOOP PULL UP (*GPWS alarm*).

Aircraft instrument: WHOOP WHOOP PULL UP (*GPWS alarm*).

Co-pilot: The airspeed indicator.

Aircraft instrument: WHOOP WHOOP PULL UP (*GPWS alarm*).

Fire service leader: De Gaulle tower from fire service leader.

Controller: Fire service leader, uh . . . the Concorde, I don't know its intentions, get yourself in position near the south doublet (*sound of switch*).

Pilot: (*unclear*).

Fire service leader: De Gaulle tower from fire service leader authorisation to enter 26 right.

Co-pilot: Le Bourget, Le Bourget, Le Bourget.

Pilot: Too late (*unclear*).

Controller: Fire service leader, correction, the Concorde is returning to runway zero nine in the opposite direction.

Pilot: No time, no (*unclear*).

Co-pilot: Negative, we're trying Le Bourget (*four switching sounds*).

Co-pilot: No (*unclear*).

Fire service leader: De Gaulle tower from fire service leader, can you give me the situation of the Concorde? (*two gongs and sound of switch followed by another switch and sounds likened to objects being moved*).

Pilot: (*unclear, sounds like exertion*).

Pilot: (*unclear, sounds like exertion*).

Pilot: (*unclear, sounds like exertion*).

The last sound was noted at 4:44:30pm and the recording ends at 4:44:31pm.

SOVIET SORROW

Russia's Tupolev Tu-144 will also be remembered for two spectacular failures with tragic consequences. The first occurred during a flying display at Le Bourget, and the other on a test flight in the Soviet Union. Both were shrouded in mystery, and to a certain degree remain so. The Concorde tragedy revived memories of a day in summer 1973, when the village of Goussainville, just under five miles (8km) from the

Concorde crash site, found itself at the receiving end of a no less deadly disaster during the Paris air show. The Concorde prototype had impressed immensely with its low flypast and steep climb, which rankled with the Soviet establishment and the crew of the competing Tupolev Tu-144. Given the history of the aircraft and the Soviets' need not to be outdone by the West, what happened on 3 June became easier to understand.

Based on reports of conversations, it later became clear that Tupolev test pilot Mikhail Kozlov was determined on that day to emulate and surpass Concorde's show-stopping performance. After an extremely fast pass at very low level, with landing gear and canards still extended, Kozlov pulled the Tu-144 into a near vertical climbing turn, but the awe felt by thousands of spectators quickly turned to horror as the aircraft began to falter at around 10,000ft (3,000m) and pitched into a steep dive. As Kozlov attempted to pull the stalled aircraft out of its dive, it began to break up, losing both its right outer wing and tailfin.

At the same time the fuel tanks in the wings ruptured, setting one of the three falling sections ablaze. Most of the burning wreckage came down on houses in Goussainville and scattered over a wide area, killing eight people on the ground, including children in their destroyed village school. Kozlov, chief engineer Benderov, and four other crew members also perished. 60 people were injured, most suffering burns, with some losing limbs. There was damage to more than 100 dwellings, 14 of which were completely destroyed.

Almost immediately, rumours began to surface about a bungled French espionage attempt. Fundamental errors by the crew and various possibilities of mechanical failures also did the rounds, but with the joint Soviet-French accident report never published, the espionage theory persisted. The Soviets intimated that in trying to avoid a prying Armée de l'Air Mirage III fighter jet, the pilot initiated hard evasive action, which exceeded the design limits of the aircraft causing it to break up. This statement was based on allegations that the French curtailed the demonstration flight at the last minute forcing the crew to improvise a landing, apparently on the wrong runway. During a second attempt, so the Soviets contended, Kozlov and his crew found themselves on a collision course with the Mirage, initiating a sequence of events leading to the overstressing of the aircraft. It was also suggested that the TV camera in the cockpit fell into the control-stick cone on the floor, inhibiting the crew from controlling the aircraft for vital seconds before the crash.

The French authorities eventually acknowledged that they had sent up a Mirage to photograph the Tu-144 in flight, without bothering to inform the Soviets, but took no responsibility for what happened subsequently.

It is believed, however, that there was no technical malfunction of the Tu-144.

A WRONG DECISION

On the afternoon of 23 May 1978, CCCP-77111, the first Tu-144D with experimental Koliesov engines, took off from Ramenskoye test centre on a test flight to Khabarovsk in the Far East. Eduard Vaganovich Elyan, as the industry test pilot, sat in the right-hand seat, with Vladislav Popov, test-pilot for GosNII, on the left. On the seats behind sat two test engineers, Chernov and Venediktov, again representing industry and operator. Aleksandr Aleksandrovich Larin, chief pilot of the Ministry of Aviation Operations Directorate (ULS MGA), was due to captain the test flight, but was ordered by the Ministry to take what turned out to be the last scheduled service to Alma-Ata. Not long into the flight, the aircraft crash-landed in a field near Moscow.

No official announcement was made, but for a time, there were rumours circulating that a fire had broken out in the left engines and had spread to the fuselage. It was said that Elyan suceeded in shutting down one or both engines, but had insufficient power to return to Ramenskoye. The aircraft came down in a field, was gutted by burning fuel and then blew apart. That something had gone drastically wrong was confirmed in the *Washington Post* three months later, which reported that a US satellite had photographed the wreckage of an SST east of Moscow. The Soviets later reported that two crew members had been killed and two more seriously injured. Elyan and Popov survived.

It was not until September 1992 when a clearer picture emerged of what happened on that fateful day. Elyan gave a brief account of the flight in *Russian Aviation*, in which he recalled the circumstances leading to the forced landing.

A fatigue crack had formed in an experimental element of the fuel system and fuel began leaking out. Apparently the engineers noticed on their instruments that there was increased fuel flow, even though the engines were functioning normally, but believed that the problem could be solved without involving the pilots. This, he said, was a fatal error of judgement. Had they done so immediately, Elyan contended that it would have been possible to return safely to the airfield.

As the engineers had not raised the alarm, Elyan proceeded to re-light the auxiliary power unit (APU) located between the engines, which was one of the tests to be carried out on that flight. The first attempt was unsuccessful, he remembered, remarking that perhaps 'fate was trying to save us from tragedy.'

On the second attempt the APU started and ignited the fuel spray as if struck by a naked match. He continued: 'When the aircraft was on fire and Popov and I were trying to choose the best landing option, I shouted to the engineers to get out of the cockpit and into the cabin. But Chernov and Venediktov stayed in their seats to the last moment. On impact, the nose gear jack-knifed and in an instant punctured the fuselage, entering it, sadly, exactly were the engineers were sitting.'

This second tragedy gave new ammunition to its opponents and sealed the fate of the Tu-144, although Elyan believes that Aeroflot was hasty in stopping passenger flights. Aleksandr Larin, who became a member of the State Accident Investigation Commission into the crash, agreed with Elyan's sentiment, but understood that the crash had undermined the faith in the aircraft, especially as the passenger service was already hanging by a thread.

SST CASUALTY RECORD

The following table summarises the three fatal accidents, which have resulted in the write-off of the aircraft to the end of December 2000. This includes one Concorde, one Tu-144, and one improved Tu-144D. Additionally, one Concorde (F-BVFD, construction number 211) was damaged in a heavy landing and withdrawn from use. There were no casualties.

C/N	REG	OPERATOR	MODEL	DATE	LOCATION	TYPE OF ACCIDENT/INCIDENT
01-02	CCCP-77102	Tupolev	Tu-144	03/06/73	Paris/Goussainville	Broke up in mid-air during violent anti-stall manoeuvre towards end of flying display, 14 killed
06-02	CCCP-77111	Tupolev	Tu-144D	23/05/78	near Ramenskoye	Fuel leak resulted in fire when APU was re-lighted in flight during test flight. Two engineers killed in subsequent heavy emergency landing
203	F-BTSA	Air France	Concorde	25/07/00	Paris/Gonesse	Crashed in flames two minutes after take-off from Paris Charles de Gaulle, killing 113 people

CONCORDE INCIDENTS

C/N	REG	OPERATOR	DATE	LOCATION	TYPE OF ACCIDENT/INCIDENT
209	F-BVFC	Air France	14/06/79	Washington DC	Blow-out of left No.5 and 6 tyres on take-off from Washington-Dulles resulted in damage from debris to No.2 engine, rupturing of three fuel tanks and severing several hydraulic lines and electrical wires. National Transportation Safety Board (NTSB) recommended that landing gear should not be retracted when wheel/tyre problems occur
211	F-BVFD	Air France	21/07/79	Washington DC	Similar. Blown tyres on take-off from Washington-Dulles, but flight is continued. Engine compressor stalled at 8,200m, probably due to foreign object damage
211	F-BVFD	Air France	?/10/79	New York	Failure of No.7 and 8 tyres on take-off from New York-JFK International. Undercarriage retracted and flight continued untroubled to Paris
216	G-BOAF	British Airways	16/09/80	Washington DC	Tyre failed on take-off at Washington-Dulles, but flight continued to London, where damage to engines and airframe was discovered
213	F-BTSD	Air France	19/02/81	Washington DC	Blow-out out of tyres on take-off from Washington-Dulles caused engine problems which forced the crew to divert to New York. One engine shut down due to vibration
214	G-BOAG	British Airways	09/08/81	New York	Tyre began to deflate during taxi and failed at 160kt, take-off abandoned. Debris from tyre and wheel caused damage to underside of port wing, fuel tank, hydraulic lines, and inboard elevons. Engines also suffered from ingestion damage
	G-	British Airways	10/10/81	North Atlantic	Computer malfunction on London-New York service forces pilot to shut one engine and land at Boston

C/N	REG	OPERATOR	DATE	LOCATION	TYPE OF ACCIDENT/INCIDENT
211	F-BVFD	Air France	27/05/82	Paris	Damaged in heavy landing and withdrawn from use. Reduced to spares on 18 December 1994
204	G-BOAC	British Airways	11/08/87	New York	All four tyres on the left main landing gear and two on the right failed on landing, causing damage to adjacent structure
	F-	Air France	?/02/89	en route	Aircraft flying from Paris to New York was forced to turn back after cracks appeared in porthole
	G-	British Airways	12/04/89	en route	Section of rudder seprated in flight
212	G-BOAE	British Airways	04/01/91	en route	Section of lower rudder separated in flight
208	G-BOAB	British Airways	21/03/92	en route	Rudder disintegrated at 55,774ft (17,000m) NE New York on flight from London
216	G-BOAF	British Airways	15/07/93	London	Main tyre burst during landing roll at London Heathrow Airport. No.3 engine stuck in reverse thrust mode, and one hydraulic system started depressurising. Tyre debris also damaged the underside of the wing and No.3 engine intake
208	G-BOAB	British Airways	25/10/93	London	Main gear wheel brake lock resulted in tyre burst while taxying at London Heathrow. Fragments of water deflector damaged wing and punctured fuel tank
214	G-BOAG	British Airways	26/05/94	New York	Emergency declared in descent and No.3 engine shut down with low oil pressure. No.2 engine also showed intermittent low oil pressure during approach and was shut down on touchdown
	G-	British Airways	?/08/94	London	Safety checks ordered after 3.9in (100mm) cracks were found on wing
	G-	British Airways	26/05/98	North Atlantic	Section of an elevon separates one hour into the flight to New York, forcing the pilot to turn back
204	G-BOAC	British Airways	08/10/98	North Atlantic	Partial separation of lower rudder during cruise phase near Newfoundland. Flight continued on to New York without incident
	G-	British Airways	24/08/99	near New York	Near miss, with two Concordes passing within 820ft (250m) vertically and 3,609ft (1,100m) horizontally of each other
	G	British Airways	?/01/00	near London	Engine failure shortly before arrival at Heathrow on flight from Barbados results in emergency landing
	G	British Airways	?/01/00	near London	Aircraft aborts pleasure trip to Bay of Biscay and returns to Heathrow when fire alarm sounds shortly after take-off
	G-	British Airways	17/03/00	Shannon	Emergency landing at Shannon, Ireland after No.3 engine shut down
	G	British Airways	23/07/00	London	Microscopic cracks are found in the wing spars of all seven Concordes, resulting in the temporary grounding of one aircraft. Air France also reports cracks in four of its Concordes, but keeps aircraft flying

10 SST PRODUCTION

BAC/AÉROSPATIALE CONCORDE

C/N	REG	MODEL	OPERATOR	FIRST FLIGHT	REMARKS
001	F-WTSS		Sud-Aviation (later Aérospatiale)	02/03/1969	French-assembled first prototype. Completed 397 flights and spent 812 hours in the air, 254 of them supersonic, before being delivered to Paris Le Bourget 19 October 1973 for permanent display at the Musée de l'Air.
002	G-BSST		BAC	09/04/1969	British-assembled second prototype. Registered to Ministry of Technology 06/05/1968 and transferred to Ministry of Aviation Supply 19 February 1971. Bought by the Science Museum 26 July 1976 and preserved at the Fleet Air Arm Museum at Yeovilton, Somerset. Spent 836 hours in the air on 438 flights, of which 173 hours were flown supersonically.
01	G-AXDN		BAC	17/12/1971	British-assembled pre-production aircraft. Registered to the Ministry of Technology 16 April 1969 and transferred to the Ministry of Aviation Supply 19 February 1971. Bought by the Imperial War Museum and delivered to Duxford Aviation Museum 20 August 1975. Flew 217 hours out of 633 supersonically, completing 269 flights.
02	F-WTSA		Aérospatiale	10/01/1973	French-assembled pre-production aircraft. Handed over to Aéroports de Paris (ADP) 26 May 1976 for public display at Paris-Orly. Logged 642 hours, 280 supersonic, on 311 flights.
201	F-WTSB	100	Aérospatiale	06/12/1973	WFU and stored at Toulouse.
202	G-BBDG	100	BAC	13/02/1974	Registered 7 August 1973 and transferred on formation of British Aerospace on 1 April 1977. WFU and stored at Filton December 1981.
203	F-WTSC F-BTSC F-BTSC F-BTSC	100 101	Aérospatiale Aérospatiale Air France Air France	31/01/1975	French-assembled production aircraft. Reregistered 28 May 1975. Leased between 6 January 1976 and 8 December 1976, and again on 11 June 1979. Converted to Model 101 and bought 23 October 1980. Crashed two minutes after take-off from Paris-Charles de Gaulle 25 July 2000. Total hours flown 11,989. Landings 3,978.
204	G-BOAC G-BOAC G-N81AC/ N81AC	102	BAC British Airways British Airways/ Braniff Airways	27/02/1975	British-assembled production aircraft, registered 3 April 1974. Delivered 13 February 1976. Registered 5 January 1979 for code-share operation between Washington and Dallas Ft Worth.

C/N	REG	MODEL	OPERATOR	FIRST FLIGHT	REMARKS
	G-BOAC		British Airways		Reregistered 11 August 1980
205	F-BVFA	101	Air France	27/10/1975	French-assembled production aircraft, delivered 19/12/75.
	N94FA		Air France/ Braniff Airways		Reregistered 12 January 1979 for code-share operation between Washington and Dallas Ft Worth.
	F-BVFA		Air France		Reregistered 1 June 1980
206	G-BOAA	102	BAC	05/11/1975	British-assembled production aircraft, registered 3/03/74.
	G-BOAA		British Airways		Delivered 14 January 1976.
	G-N94AA/ N94AA		British Airways/ Braniff Airways		Reregistered 12 January 1979 for code-share operation between Washington and Dallas Ft Worth.
	G-BOAA		British Airways		Reregistered 28 July 1980.
207	F-BVFB	101	Air France	06/03/1976	French-assembled production aircraft, delivered 8/04/76.
	N94FB		Air France/ Braniff Airways		Reregistered 12 January 1979 for code-share operation between Washington and Dallas Ft Worth.
	F-BVFB		Air France		Reregistered 1 June 1980.
208	G-BOAB	102	BAC	18/05/1976	British-assembled production aircraft, registered 3/03/74.
	G-BOAB		British Airways		Delivered 30 September 1976.
	G-N94AB/ N94AB		British Airways/ Braniff Airways		Reregistered 12 January 1979 for code-share operation between Washington and Dallas Ft Worth.
	G-BOAB		British Airways		Reregistered 17 September 1980.
209	F-BVFC	101	Air France	09/07/1976	French-assembled production aircraft, delivered 3/08/76.
	N94FC		Air France/ Braniff Airways		Reregistered 12 January 1979 for code-share operation between Washington and Dallas Ft Worth.
	F-BVFC		Air France		Reregistered 1 June 1980.
210	G-BOAD	102	BAC	25/08/1976	British-assembled production aircraft, registered 9/05/75.
	G-BOAD		British Airways		Delivered 6 December 1976.
	G-N94AD/ N94AD		British Airways/ Braniff Airways		Reregistered 5 January 1979 for code-share operation between Washington and Dallas Ft Worth.
	G-BOAD		British Airways		Reregistered 19 June 1980.
211	F-BVFD	101	Air France	10/02/1977	French-assembled production aircraft, delivered 26/03/77.
	N94FD		Air France/ Braniff Airways		Reregistered 12 January 1979 for code-share operation between Washington and Dallas Ft Worth.
	F-BVFD		Air France		Reregistered 1 June 1980. Damaged in heavy landing 27/05/82 and withdrawn from use. Reduced to spares 18/12/94.
212	G-BOAE	102	BAC	17/03/1977	British-assembled production aircraft, registered 9/05/75.
	G-BOAE		British Aerospace		New name 1 April 1977.
	G-BOAE		British Airways		Delivered 20 July 1977.

C/N	REG	MODEL	OPERATOR	FIRST FLIGHT	REMARKS
	G-N94AE/ N94AE		British Airways/ Braniff Airways		Reregistered 5 January 1979 for code-share operation between Washington and Dallas Ft Worth.
	G-BOAE		British Airways		Reregistered 1 July 1980.
213	F-WJAM	101	Aérospatiale	26/06/1978	French-assembled production aircraft.
	F-BTSD		Aérospatiale		Reregistered 4 September 1978.
	F-BTSD		Air France		Leased 18 September 1978.
	N94SD		Air France/ Braniff Airways		Reregistered 12 January 1979 for code-share operation between Washington and Dallas Ft Worth.
	F-BTSD		Aérospatiale		Returned and reregistered 12 March 1979.
	F-BTSD		Air France		Leased 9 May 1980 and bought 23 October 1980.
214	G-BKFW	102	British Aerospace	21/04/1978	British-assembled production aircraft, registered 2/01/78.
	G-BFKW		British Airways		Delivered 6 February 1980.
	G-BOAG		British Airways		Reregistered 9 February 1981.
215	F-WJAN	101	Aérospatiale	26/12/1978	French-assembled production aircraft.
	F-BVFF		Air France		Reregistered and delivered 23 October 1980.
216	G-BFKX	102	British Aerospace	20/04/1979	British-assembled production aircraft, registered 27/01/78.
	G-N94AF/ G-BOAF		British Airways/ Braniff Airways		Reregistered 14 December 1979 for code-share operation between Washington and Dallas Ft Worth.
	G-N94AF/ G-BOAF		British Airways		Delivered 9 June 1980.
	G-BOAF		British Airways		Reregistered 12 June 1980.

TUPOLEV TU-144

C/N	REG	MODEL	OPERATOR	FIRST FLIGHT	REMARKS
44-00	CCCP-68001		Tupolev	31/12/1968	First prototype and first supersonic transport aircraft to fly. Made international debut at Paris Air Show in June 1971 with '826' painted on forward fuselage. Broken up.
44-01?	CCCP-68002		Tupolev		Believed second prototype, although no photographic evidence exists. The subject of rumours of a heavy landing, with undercarriage going through wing.
044			Tupolev		Probably static test specimen.
01-1	CCCP-77101		Tupolev		First production aircraft.
01-02	CCCP-77102		Tupolev		Flown to the Paris Air Show in June 1973 with '451' painted on forward fuselage. Crashed during air display on 3 June.

C/N	REG	MODEL	OPERATOR	FIRST FLIGHT	REMARKS
01-03			Tupolev		Static test cell.
01-04			Tupolev		Cell for resonance tests.
02-01	CCCP-77103		Tupolev		
02-02	CCCP-77104		Tupolev		Believed same aircraft as that appearing at the 1975 Paris Air Show as CCCP-77144 with '361' painted on forward fuselage.
03-01	CCCP-77105		Tupolev		Seen at Moscow-Domodedovo in 1978. Re-engined with Koliesov RT-36-51A variable-cycle engines.
04-01	CCCP-77106		Tupolev/Aeroflot		Used on route-proving flights between Moscow and Alma-Ata from 26/12/75. Retired to Monino in 1980.
04-02	CCCP-77107		Tupolev		Seen at Moscow-Domododevo in 1978.
05-01	CCCP-77108		Tupolev		Seen at Moscow-Domododevo in 1978.
05-02	CCCP-77109		Tupolev/Aeroflot		Operated first commercial service between Moscow to Alma Ata on 1/11/77. Later flown to Novosibirsk for static tests.
05-03			Tupolev		Probably static test specimen.
06-01	CCCP-77110		Tupolev		Made appearance at Paris Air Show in June 1977 with '345' painted on forward fuselage. On display in Ulyanovsk.
06-02	CCCP-77111	D	Tupolev	30/11/1974	First improved 'D' model with Koliesov RT-36-51A engine. Burnt out after crash landing in field near Ramenskoye on 23 May 1978.
07-01	CCCP-77112	D	Tupolev		
08-01	CCCP-77113	D	Tupolev		
08-02	CCCP-77114	D	Tupolev		Possibly aircraft '101' used to establish international speed and distance records in July 1983.
	RA-77114	LL	Tupolev/NASA		Reregistered and restored as flying laboratory and re-engined with Kutznetsov NK-321 afterburning turbofans. Used as flying testbed in Russia by NASA as part of its High-Speed Research Program (HSR), carrying out 19 research flight, flown by Russian crews between July 1995 and February 1998, and seven flights by American crews between September 1998 and April 1999. Programme halted when NASA abandoned further HSR work.
09-01	CCCP-77115	D	Tupolev		at Voronezh.
09-02	CCCP-77116	D	Tupolev		at Voronezh.

11 SST Chronology

25 February 1954 British experts meet at the Royal Aircraft Establishment (RAE) in Farnborough to discuss supersonic transport feasibility.

1954/55 US studies start into supersonic transport (SST).

1956 Serious SST research begins in Britain and France.

5 November 1956 First meeting takes place of British Supersonic Aircraft Transport Committee (STAC).

1957 French Government invites aerospace companies to submit design proposals for an SST.

January 1958 Boeing establishes SST research programme.

9 March 1959 STAC recommends detailed design of two supersonic airliners, one with a speed of Mach 1.2 and a faster Mach 2.
June Lockheed presents Mach 3 SST design to the Institute of Aeronautical Sciences in Los Angeles.
18 October Myasishchev M-50 heavy supersonic bomber makes its first flight in the Soviet Union, giving rise to the M-53 project studies for a supersonic transport aircraft.

1959-61 Feasibility and design studies are underway in Britain on the BAC 223 and in France on the Super-Caravelle. Preliminary Anglo-French discussions on Supersonic Transport (SST) requirements lead to investigation into possible collaboration.

1960 British Airways receives its first supersonic passenger reservation.

1961 Russian airline Aeroflot issues requirement for supersonic transport aircraft.
8 June First discussions are held in Paris between the British Aircraft Corporation (BAC) and Sud-Aviation.
July SST steering group established in the United States comprising the Federal Aviation Agency (FAA), the National Aeronautics and Space Administration (NASA), and members from the Defense Department.
10 July Discussions between French and British manufacturers continue at Weybridge.
August US Congress appropriates $11 million for FAA SST research.
September Project Horizon report recommends US SST development.
November FAA requests industry proposals for SST research; Supersonic Transport Advisory Group (STAG) is formed.

January 1962 The results of an investigation into the

parameters for a civil SST, based on M-53 project, is published in the Soviet Union.
14 May Wind tunnel tests are carried out in the Soviet Union on a M-53 model.
25 October First Anglo-French Mach 2.2 aircraft specification is published, covering both medium-range and long-range versions.
October US Congress appropriates $20 million for continued research into US SST.
29 November Anglo-French intergovernmental agreement is signed for joint study, development and manufacture of supersonic aircraft.
December STAG recommends development of US SST.

1963 Preliminary design for a 100-seat SST is discussed with key airlines.
January US SST review committee is formed, chaired by Vice President Lyndon B Johnson.
13 January French President Charles de Gaulle mentions the name 'Concorde' when referring to the Anglo-French supersonic aircraft. UK prefers 'Concord' spelling.
May First metal is cut for test specimens.
June Sales options for Concorde are signed by BOAC and Air France.
3 June Pan American World Airways signs first sales option for Concorde.
5 June President John F Kennedy announces US supersonic transport programme.
July SST development office formed within FAA.
16 July Soviet Presidium votes to proceed with the construction of a SST.
26 July Development contract is given to the Tupolev OKB.
August US President John F Kennedy appoints special advisors on SST financing.
15 August FAA invites bids from American industry to begin SST work in earnest.
November Following assassination of President Kennedy, US Congress votes $60 million for SST.
December US report on SST financing is submitted to President Johnson.

January 1964 US industry submits initial design proposals.
May Medium-range version abandoned and enlarged long-range version announced featuring a 20 percent increase in wing area, increased fuel, and greater take-off weight of 150 tonnes. This design is later frozen for prototype construction.
May President Johnson orders further design work, economic studies and sonic boom research.
June First US design contracts awarded to Boeing, Lockheed and North American.
July Rolls-Royce SNECMA Olympus 593 'D' (Derivative) turbojet engine makes first run at Bristol.

April 1965 First metal is cut for Concorde prototypes.

May 130-seat pre-production Concorde design is announced.

June Model of Soviet Tu-144 SST exhibited at Paris Air Show.

July FAA announces 18-month design competition.

October Sub-assembly begins of first Concorde prototypes.

November First run of Olympus 593 'B' (Big) engine at Bristol.

March 1966 Centre fuselage/wing section for static and thermal testing is delivered to CEAT in Toulouse.

April Final assembly of Concorde prototype 001 begins at Toulouse.

June First test-bed run of complete Olympus 593 engine and variable geometry exhaust assembly completed at Melun-Villaroche in France. Concorde flight simulator is commissioned at Toulouse.

July FAA requests Phase 3 proposals.

August Final assembly of Concorde 002 begins at Filton, Bristol.

September Vulcan bomber flying testbed with Olympus 593 makes its first flight. Olympus 593 first run in Cell 3 high-altitude facility at the National Gas Turbine Establishment (NGTE) at Pyestock, England.

September US industry submits latest proposals; Congress appropriates $280 million for 1966-67.

October Olympus 593 achieves 156.6kN (dry) thrust on test at Bristol, exceeding 'Stage 1' requirements.

December Fuselage and nose section delivered to RAE (Royal Aircraft Establishment) Farnborough for fatigue testing.

31 December FAA selects Boeing as prime airframe manufacturer for the US SST, and General Electric for the engines.

February 1967 Full-scale Concorde interior mock-up presented to customer airlines at Filton.

April Complete Olympus 593 engine first test-run is completed at high-altitude chamber at Saclay, France.

29 April President Johnson gives go-ahead for US SST.

May Concorde options reach 74 from 16 airlines.

1 May Contract is signed for two prototypes of the Boeing 2707.

August Concorde 001 undergoes resonance testing at Toulouse.

October US Congress appropriates $142.4 million funds for 1967-68.

11 December Concorde prototype 001 F-WTSS is rolled out at Toulouse. Name of Concorde is officially adopted by the British.

January 1968 Vulcan Olympus 593 testbed logs first 100 flying hours. SNECMA variable-geometry exhaust assembly for Olympus 593 engine is cleared at Melun-Villaroche for flight in Concorde prototypes.

February British Government announces provision of a £125m loan to launch production aircraft and engines.

February Boeing requests more time to validate its variable-geometry design.

4 February Preliminary engine testing takes place on Concorde prototype 001.

18 April MiG-21I Analog aircraft makes its first flight.

20 August Concorde prototype 001 undertakes first taxi trials.

September Second Concorde prototype 002 is rolled out at Filton.

October Boeing decides on fixed-wing design.

December Olympus 593 ground testing reaches 5,000 hours.

8 December Boeing announces new fixed-delta 2707-300.

31 December Tupolev Tu-144 (CCCP-68001) maiden flight at Zhukovsky, powered by Kuznetsov NK-144 turbofan engines, becoming first supersonic transport aircraft to fly.

January 1969 Boeing submits new variable-geometry wing design to FAA.

8 January Tupolev Tu-144 makes second flight and begins test programme.

29 January New US President Richard Nixon sets up committee to investigate SST.

17 February Concorde 001 completes high-speed taxi trials.

2 March Concorde prototype 001 (F-WTSS) makes 29-minute maiden flight, taking off from Toulouse. Crew comprises André Turcat, Jacques Guignard, Michel Rétif and Henri Perrier.

March Governmental authority obtained for a total of nine Concorde airframes — two prototypes, two pre-production, two ground test airframes, and three production aircraft.

9 April British-assembled Concorde Prototype 002 (G-BSST) makes its first flight from Filton to Fairford, piloted by Brian Trubshaw and John Cochrane, assisted by flight engineer Brian Watts.

June Both Concorde prototypes make their first public appearance at the Paris Air Show.

BELOW: Magnificent photo-call by four British Airways Concordes in Union Flag markings.

5 June Tupolev Tu-144 prototype achieves Mach 1.0.

July Annular combustion system to reduce exhaust smoke is specified for all subsequent Concordes.

23 September President Nixon gives go-ahead for Boeing 2707-300.

1 October Concorde (001) flies for the first time at supersonic speed (Mach 1).

8-10 November First airline pilots from Air France, BOAC, Pan Am and TWA take the controls of prototype 001. Concorde reaches Mach 1.3.

December Governments authorise three more production Concordes — numbers 4, 5 and 6.

December US Congress approves $85 million for SST prototype development.

February 1970 Longest single test run of 300 hours carried out on Olympus 593 engine — equivalent to nearly 100 trans-Atlantic flights.

25 March Concorde 002 achieves Mach 1 for the first time.

April US SST programme is transferred from FAA to Department of Transportation.

10 April British Minister of Technology Anthony Wedgwood Benn makes first VIP flight in Concorde 002.

May New TRA (Thrust Reverser Aft) engine nozzle specified for production Concordes.

May US House of Representatives rejects amendment to delete $290 million from SST funds.

21 May Tupolev Tu-144 makes public debut at Moscow-Sheremetyevo Airport.

26 May Tupolev Tu-144 reaches Mach 2.0 on 45th flight, later up to Mach 2.4.

August Concorde flights resumed with Olympus 593-3B engines and auto-controlled air intakes.

1 September Concorde 002 makes first flight over British West Coast test corridor.

13 September Concorde 002 appears at Farnborough Air Show and goes on to make first landing at an international airport at London Heathrow.

4 November Mach 2, twice the speed of sound, is reached for the first time (001).

12 November Concorde 002 first achieves Mach 2.

December US Senate passes Proxmire amendment to delete SST funds from transportation appropriations. Concorde design changes announced.

January 1971 100th Concorde supersonic flight is completed. US Congress approves funding to 30 March 1971.

18 March US House of Representatives votes to delete all SST funds.

24 March US Congress halts US supersonic transport programme.

April Four more production Concordes (numbers 7-10) are authorised, together with the purchase of long-lead materials for the next six aircraft (11-16).

7 May French President Georges Pompidou becomes the first head of state to fly supersonic.

13 May Concorde 001 makes first automatic landing.

25 May The first international flight is made when Concorde routes Paris–Dakar, piloted by Jean Pinet, completing the 2,796 miles (4,500km) flight in 2h 35min.

June Concorde flight test time reaches 500 hours; engine testing totals 10,000 hours. Tupolev Tu-144 is shown for the first time outside the Soviet Union at the Paris Air Show.

July Airline pilots fly Concorde at Mach 2.

16 July British Minister for Aerospace Frank Corfield flies in Concorde 002.

August Concorde completes 100th flight at Mach 2. Flight clearance obtained for Olympus 593-4 engine.

4-18 September Concorde prototype 001 undertakes trouble-free tour to Brazil and Argentinia.

20 September First pre-production Concorde 01 rolled out at Filton.

12 November HRH Princess Anne visits the Concorde assembly hall at BAC Filton.

December Further design changes are made to Concorde, including a new intake control system and airworthiness modifications.

2 December Testing of the new SNECMA TRA 28 nozzle begins at the Saclay test facility in France.

7 December Basic sales price of £13m for Concorde agreed in Paris by British Minister for Aerospace Frederick Corfield and the French Minister of Transport Jean Chamant.

10 December Continued British Government support for Concorde announced after a flight in 002 by the British Secretary of State for Trade and Industry, John Davies, and Minister of Defence Lord Carrington.

BELOW: Concorde should soon be soaring back into the air.

3 December French president Georges Pompidou flies in Concorde to the Azores for meeting with US President Richard Nixon.

4 December FAA states that Concorde will be within American airport noise limits.

7 December First pre-production Concorde 01 (G-AXDN) makes maiden flight from Filton to Fairford.

21 December All three flying Concordes — 001, 002 and 01 — make simultaneous test flights.

22 December Pricing formula for initial Concorde customer airlines is announced in British Parliament.

6 January 1972 All three Concordes land at Fairford.

12 January HRH The Duke of Edinburgh pilots Concorde 002 during a two-hour supersonic mission.

7 February Concorde 002 flies with production landing gear.

12 February Pre-production Concorde 01 reaches supersonic speed.

April First Olympus 593 Mk.602 is delivered to Toulouse for 02, total Olympus running time exceeds 20,000 hours.

7 April Concorde 001 reaches 500hrs on its 245th flight.

13 April The British and French governments authorise production of a further six aircraft (11-16).

22-3 April Concorde 002 appears at Hanover Air Show, Germany.

5 May Concorde 001 flies from Toulouse to Tangier.

5 May HRH Princess Margaret, the Duke of Kent, Prince William of Gloucester and Lord Snowdon fly in 002.

18 May The three Concordes — 001, 002 and 01 — complete 1,000 flying hours.

19 May British Prime Minister Edward Heath flies in Concorde 002.

25 May BOAC announces intention to order five Concordes.

2 June-1 July Concorde prototype 002 makes world sales tour to 12 countries in the Middle East, Far East and Australia.

24 July Representatives of the Civil Aviation Administration of China (CAAC) sign a preliminary purchase agreement with Aérospatiale in Paris for two Concordes.

28 July Air France and BOAC place first firm order for Concorde, signing up for four and five aircraft respectively.

August First production Tu-144 (CCCP77101) makes maiden flight.

10 August Concorde 01 returns to Filton for modifications to bring it up to near full-production standard; includes Olympus 593 Mk 602 power plants and intakes.

28 August China signs preliminary purchase agreement with BAC in Beijing for a third Concorde.

4-10 September Concorde 002 participates daily at the flying display at the Farnborough Air Show.

14 September Government approval is given for the procurement of long-lead materials for a further six aircraft (17-22).

20 September Tu-144 CCCP77101 makes high-speed flight from Moscow to Tashkent, at an average speed of 1,678mph (2,700 km/h).

28 September Second pre-production Concorde 02 is rolled out at Toulouse.

5 October Iran Air signs preliminary purchase agreement for two Concordes, and takes out option for a third.

December French delegation visits Tu-144 production facility at Voronezh.

11 December British Government approves increase in production loan from £125m to £350m.

10 January 1973 Second pre-production Concorde 02 (F-WTSA) takes off for the first time at Toulouse, fitted with the Olympus 593 Mk.602 engines.

22 January-24 February Concorde 002 undertakes hot-and-high airfield performance trials at Johannesburg, South Africa and demonstrates the aircraft at Cape Town.

31 January Pan Am and TWA drop their Concorde options, but leave the door open for further proposals.

23 February Concorde 02 makes 3,728 mile (6,000km) roundtrip between Toulouse and Reykjavik in Iceland — equivalent to Paris–New York — in 3h 27min, of which 2h 9min are flown at Mach 2.

March Sales option system is abandoned.

3 March Concorde 02 makes 3,902 mile (6,280km) roundtrip between Toulouse and West Africa — equivalent to Frankfurt–New York — in 3h 38min.

15 March Concorde 01 returns from Filton to Fairford for major modifications.

3 June Tupolev Tu-144 CCCP-77102 stalls and crashes at Le Bourget during flying display at Paris Air Show.

30 June Concorde 001 makes 'Sun eclipse' flight over Africa, tracking the eclipse between Las Palmas in the Canaries and Fort Lamy (now N'djamena) in Chad for 75 minutes.

9 July Concorde 002 begins three-week trial at Torrejon, Madrid, Spain.

20 September Concorde 02 makes first landing in the United States, touching down at Dallas Ft Worth after stopovers at Las Palmas and Caracas.

18 September Concorde 02 makes first US visit for opening of Dallas/Ft Worth Airport, via Las Palmas and Caracas.

26 September Concorde makes first trans-Atlantic crossing, flying Washington–Paris-Orly in a record 3h 33min.

19 October Concorde 001 makes last flight to Paris-Le Bourget for display at the Musée de l'Air, after completing 812 hours in the air, 254 at supersonic speed.

6 December First production Concorde 201 (F-WTSB) flies at Toulouse.

1974 Aérospatiale begins studies into an advanced successor to Concorde.

7-19 February Concorde undertakes cold weather trials at Anchorage and Fairbanks in Alaska.

13 February Second production Concorde 202 (G-BBDG) makes its first flight from Filton to Fairford.

May Aeroflot begins route proving flights with the Tu-144.

27 May Concorde 02 begins trial flights between Paris and Rio de Janeiro, Brazil.

5 June Concorde 02 completes the 18,240 km Paris–Rio de Janeiro–Paris roundtrip in one day, spending 11h 20min in the air.

17 June Concorde completes Paris–Boston–Paris roundtrip in one day, in 6h 18min flying time, taking five minutes less time than a Boeing 747 on the Paris–Boston leg.

25 June Concorde static test specimen tested to destruction at CEAT after completing design load tests.

19 July Britain and France agree initial production run of 16 Concordes.

7 August-2 September Concorde 202 undergoes hot weather trials in Persian Gulf and runway response tests at Singapore, and makes first demonstration tour in the Middle East, visiting Doha, Kuwait, Abu Dhabi, Dubai and Muscat on 27 August.

3 September Concorde 202 leaves Bahrain for runway response trials at Singapore.

12 September Concorde flight testing reaches 3,000 hours.

1 October New interior design incorporated into cabin mock-up.

20-28 October Concorde 02 tours Mexico, US West Coast, Colombia, Peru and Venezuela.

21 October Supersonic flight time reaches 1,000 hours.

7 November Concorde 01 flies from Fairford to Moses Lake, Washington, via Bangor, for de-icing trials, making fastest civil crossing of the Atlantic.

30 November Heavily-modified Tupolev Tu-144D with Koliesov RT-36 variable-cycle engines makes its first flight.

26 December Tu-144 (CCCP77106) begins regular cargo flights between Moscow and Alma-Ata.

31 January 1975 Production Concorde 203 (F-WTSC) makes its first flight.

11 February Passenger evacuation certification trials completed.

26 February Concorde 01 flies to Nairobi, Kenya for tropical icing trials.

27 February Production Concorde 204 (G-BOAC) maiden flight.

28 February Concorde 202 begins three weeks of certification trials at Madrid.

3 March FAA publishes Draft Environmental Impact Statement (EIS) on proposed US operations by Concorde.

28 May-2 August Following award of a special-category Certificate of Airworthiness by the French SGAC, Concorde 203 (re-registered F-BTSC) makes 125 endurance flights to Rio de Janeiro, Gander and Caracas, covering a total of 367,914 miles (592,100km).

30 May Concorde 201 participates in flying display at Paris air show; 202 on static display.

9 June Concorde 201 starts endurance flying.

30 June Special-category CofA awarded to Concorde 204 by UK Civil Aviation Authority (CAA).

7 July-13 September Concorde 204 undertakes 130 endurance flights to Bahrain, Bombay, Singapore, Melbourne, Beirut, Damascus and Gander, covering a distance of 326,220 miles (525,000km).

1 September Concorde 204 operates four North Atlantic crossings during the same day.

3-6 October Concorde 02 at inauguration of the new international terminal at Montréal Mirabel Airport, flying London–Ottawa in 4h 6min, and Montréal–Paris in 3h 50min.

9 October Concorde obtains French Certificate of Airworthiness.

14 October Air France and British Airways open reservations for scheduled Concorde services.

25 October Production Concorde 205 (F-BVFA) makes its first flight at Toulouse.

5 November Production Concorde 206 (G-BOAA) flies for first time at Filton.

13 November FAA publishes final Environmental Impact Statement (EIS).

5 December Concorde receives Certificate of Airworthiness from the UK Civil Aviation Authority (CAA).

19 December Air France takes delivery of its first Concorde, registered F-BVFA.

26 December Tu-144 begins route proving flights between Moscow and Alma Ata.

5 January 1976 Public hearing on Concorde held in Washington, DC, by US Secretary of Transportation, William T Coleman.

6 January Air France receives its second Concorde (203, F-BTSC).

15 January British Airways takes delivery of its first Concorde (206, G-BOAA).

21 January At 1140 GMT, Air France Concorde No.5 and British Airways Concorde No.6 take off simultaneously on the world's first scheduled supersonic services. The Air France service is operated from Paris to Rio de Janeiro, via Dakar; British Airways flies from London to Bahrain.

4 February US Transportation secretary William T Coleman makes decision to allow trial services into the US for 16 months, allowing for 12 months of noise measurements and four months of analysis of results.

13 February British Airways receives its second Concorde (204, G-BOAC); UK Treasury authorises free transfer of Concorde 002 to Science Museum and 01 to Duxford Aviation Society.

6 March Concorde 207 (F-BVFB) makes its first flight.

11 March Concorde is banned from John F Kennedy International Airport for six months by the Port Authority of New York and New Jersey, while it observes operations at Paris, London and Washington and studies noise levels.

8 April Air France receives its third Concorde (207, F-BVFB).

9 April Air France inaugurates Concorde services to Caracas, the capital of Venezuela, with a technical stop at Santa Maria, Azores. Distance flown is 4,735 miles (7,620km).

18 May Concorde 208 takes off from Filton on its first flight, reaching Mach 2.05 at 19,200 m.

24 May Air France and British Airways add Concorde services to Washington, DC, on the same day.

26 May French-built pre-production Concorde 02 is handed over to Aéroports de Paris (ADP) for public display at Paris-Orly Airport, after flying from Toulouse with the same crew, which had manned it on its maiden flight.

28 May Australian Minister for Transport, Peter Nixon, gives approval for Concorde to begin regular services to Australia. British Airways planned to begin services to Melbourne in February 1977, but never started.

June Aérospatiale abandons work on Concorde successor.

26 June British PM James Callaghan flies from London to economic summit meeting in Puerto Rico in a chartered British Airways Concorde. The 5,220 mile (8,400km) flight is longest supersonic flight to date, taking 4h 10min.

26 July British-built Concorde prototype 002 retired to the Fleet Air Arm Museum at Yeovilton, Somerset. Handed over by Industry Secretary Gerald Kaufman after 400+ flights, of which nearly 200 were supersonic.

9 July Concorde 209 (F-BVFC) makes first flight at Toulouse.

3 August Air France accepts its fourth Concorde (209, F-BVFC).

5 August Concorde 210, G-BOAD, makes first flight at Filton.

0 September British Airways receives its third Concorde (208, G-BOAB).

November Concorde 203 leaves on Far East demonstration tour.

0 November Fairford flight test base is closed, all operations transferred to Filton.

December British Airways takes delivery of its fourth Concorde (210, G-BOAD).

December Air France returns Concorde 203 to Aérospatiale.

10 February 1977 Concorde 211, F-BVFD, makes its maiden flight at Toulouse.

22 February Tupolev Tu-144 makes first flight from Moscow to Khabarovsk, a distance of 3,902 miles (6,280km).

9 March British PM James Callaghan flies to Washington on Concorde.

17 March Concorde 212, G-BOAE, flies for first time at Filton.

26 March Air France takes delivery of Concorde 211, F-BVFD, bringing fleet back up to four aircraft.

20 July British Airways receives its fifth Concorde (212, G-BOAE).

20 August Pre-production Concorde 01 is retired to Duxford, under the care of the Imperial War Museum.

September Aeroflot decides to start commercial supersonic services in November.

19 October Concorde 201 begins proving flights into New York's John F Kennedy International Airport.

26 October British Airways and Singapore Airlines announce agreement for joint London–Singapore flights, via Bahrain.

1 November Aeroflot inaugurates commercial services with the Tupolev Tu-144 between Moscow and Alma Ata.

2 November On the occasion of the silver jubilee, HM Queen Elizabeth II flies on Concorde from Barbados and London, after completing an official state visit to Canada and the Caribbean. The 4,176 mile (6,720km) flight takes 3h 45min.

22 November Air France and British Airways begin simultaneous scheduled services to New York from Paris and London.

9 December British Airways extends its Bahrain service to Singapore in conjunction with Singapore Airlines, flying supersonically over the Indian Ocean. Service is suspended after only three flights because of overflying ban by Malaysia.

21 April 1978 Concorde 214, G-BFKW, makes its first flight at Filton.

23 May Tupolev Tu-144D crashes in field near Ramenskoye with the loss of the two flight engineers and burns out.

6 June Aeroflot ceases its Tupolev Tu-144 supersonic services following the crash of the second aircraft two weeks earlier.

26 June Concorde 213, F-BTSD, makes first flight at Toulouse.

10 August British Airways carries 100,000th Concorde passenger.

18 September Air France receives its fifth Concorde (213, F-BTSD).

BELOW: Tailpiece.

G-BOAF

26 December Concorde 215, F-WJAN, makes first flight at Toulouse.

9 January 1979 Concorde obtains its US type certificate.
12 January US airline Braniff, in co-operation with Air France and British Airways, begins subsonic Washington DC–Dallas Ft Worth services as an extension from the Paris and London flights.
24 January British Airways and Singapore Airlines resume Bahrain– Singapore service.
12 February HM The Queen and Prince Philip fly Concorde G-BOAE to Kuwait at the start of a three-week Middle East tour; continuing later to Bahrain and Riyadh.
22 February British Government announces write-off of British Airways Concorde purchase costs; government is to receive 80 percent of operating surplus.
3 April British Government announces that two unsold British-assembled Concordes are to be allocated to British carrier(s).
20 April Last production Concorde (216, G-BFKX) makes its first flight at Filton.
11 June Concorde 203, F-BTSC, is redelivered to Air France.
23 June Improved Tupolev Tu-144D makes a Moscow–Khabarovsk flight with A A Tupolev on board, covering the 3,843 mile (6,185km) distance in 3h 21min.
20 September Air France extends its Paris–Washington Concorde service to Mexico City.
21 September British and French Governments announce that unsold aircraft and spare engines are to be placed with Air France and British Airways.
16 December British Airways Concorde makes London–New York flight in record 2h 59min 36sec.

6 February 1980 British Airways receives its sixth Concorde (214, G-BFKW).
1 June Services from Paris and London to Dallas Ft Worth are discontinued.
13 June British Airways receives its seventh Concorde (216, G-BFKX).
17 July Sir George Edwards opens Science Museum Concorde exhibition at Yeovilton, including Concorde 002, H.P.115 and BAC 212.
23 October Air France receives its seventh Concorde (215, F-BVFF).
1 November British Airways London–Singapore service is discontinued.

1981 A decision is taken in Moscow not to proceed with commercial services with the Tupolev Tu-144D.
15 January House of Commons Industry and Trade Committee announces short inquiry into rising costs of Concorde.
21 January Concorde completes five years of service, accumulating 50,500 hours on 15,800 flights, and carrying 700,000 passengers.
28 January British Airways, British Aerospace and Rolls-Royce give evidence on Concorde to Commons Industry and Trade Committee.
4 February British Minister of State for Industry, Norman Tebbit, gives evidence on Concorde to Industry and Trade Committee.
29 March Air France discontinues its direct supersonic

Paris–Washington flights, serving the capital as an extension of its New York service.
14 April Industry and Trade Committee publishes its report on Concorde, expressing dissatisfaction with costs and suggesting that the project 'had acquired a life of its own and was out of control.' It urges efforts to ensure that costs are shared equally with France.
14 July In its reply to the committee's report, the government dismisses criticisms of forecasts as 'unwarranted', and confirms taking action to reduce costs and 'to press for the implementation of the equal sharing provisions of the 1962 Anglo-French Agreement'.
11 September British and French Governments commission joint studies on future of Concorde.
29 October British and French ministers meet in London to study three options for future of Concorde proposed by officials. The three options are cancellation from 1 April 1982, a phased rundown, and indefinite continuation.
2 December British Government review of relative costs of Concorde cancellation/continuation presented to Parliament by the Department of Trade and Industry.
9 December Officials from the UK Department of Trade and Industry give evidence to the Industry and Trade Committee.

20 January 1982 Air France announces that it will cease its Rio and Caracas services.
February The Industry and Trade Committee publishes further report on Concorde saying that the government must ensure the British taxpayer 'does not have to provide more money'.
1 April Air France stops its Paris–Rio de Janeiro and Paris–Caracas Concorde services because of heavy losses.
1 May British Airways creates separate Concorde Division, to develop its supersonic charter activities.
6 May British and French ministers meet in Paris to discuss Concorde.
1 November Air France discontinues the New York–Washington and Mexico City extensions.

27 March 1984 British Airways extends London–Washington Concorde service three times a week to Miami.
August Aeroflot confirms that it has ceased supersonic flights.

13 February 1985 First Concorde charter flight leaves London for Sydney, reaching the Australian city in 17h 30min.
28 March A British Airways Concorde flies from London to Cape Town in 8h 8min.

1986 NASA issues contracts to Boeing and McDonnell Douglas as part of its HSCT studies.
8 November First Concorde round the world flight departs London and returns via New York, San Francisco, Honolulu Guam, Hong Kong, Bali and Cairo. The 28,249 mile (45,463km) trip is covered in 29h 59min flying time.
2 December An Air France Concorde makes 18 day round the world flight from and to Paris via New York, Oakland, Honolulu, Papeete, Sydney, Jakarta, Bangkok, Colombo and Bahrain.

1989 Gulfstream Aerospace and Sukhoi Design Bureau co-operate in design of the S-21 Supersonic Business Jet (SSBJ).

May 1990 International study group is formed to explore issues involved in developing a second-generation SST. The group comprises Aérospatiale, Boeing, British Aerospace, Deutsche Airbus and McDonnell Douglas. Alenia and Tupolev join in 1991.

1991 S-21 SSBJ project is abandoned.

January British Airways ceases the Washington–Miami extension of its Concorde schedule.

June Tupolev OKB exhibits model of new supersonic transport aircraft at Paris Air Show, the Tu-244, but no further progress reported.

April 1994 Aérospatiale, British Aerospace and Dasa sign MoU for a jointly-funded European Supersonic Research Programme (ESRP).

12 October An Air France Concorde makes a record round the world flight in east/west direction in 33h 1min.

1 November British Airways suspends its London–Washington Concorde service, but begins regular winter charters to Barbados.

16 August 1995 An Air France Concorde makes another record round the world flight, this time in west/east direction in 31h 27min.

17 March 1996 Tupolev Tu-144LL flying laboratory (RA-77114) is rolled out at Zhukovsky.

2 April Air France Concorde F-BTSD is rolled out painted in Pepsi colours for launch of new corporate identity.

June NASA teamed with US and Russian aerospace industries begin joint international high-speed research programme in the Tu-144LL.

September 1997 Dassault announces feasibility studies into a three-engined SSBJ based on the Falcon.

January 1999 NASA abandons its High-Speedresearch (HSR) programme.

March Dassault discontinues its studies into a SSBJ.

14 May 2000 An Air France Concorde is leased by US lingerie firm Victoria's Secret for promotional flight from New York to Nice.

25 July Chartered Air France Concorde F-BTSC crashes two minutes after take-off from Paris Charles de Gaulle Airport, killing all 109 people on board plus four on the ground. The tragedy is Concorde's first fatal accident. Air France stops all Concorde flights pending the results of the accident investigation.

16 August Concorde Certificate of Airworthiness is suspended.

21 September Air France Concorde F-BVFC is ferried back to Paris after being stranded at New York JF Kennedy. Special authorisation obtained from French DGAC.

2001 Alexei Tupolev, chief designer on the Tu-144, and Brian Trubshaw, who flew the first British-built Concorde, both die.

BELOW: Modified British Airways Concorde G-BOAF made a first test flight on 17 July 2001, almost a year after the fatal Paris crash. Featuring new Kevlar fuel tank linings, strengthened wiring around the undercarriage area and new tyres, a series of tests were expected to lead to a reinstatement of the aircraft's operating certificate and resumption of scheduled services by the autumn.

INDEX